Canadian Wildflowers

Canadian Wildflowers
Through the Seasons

MARY FERGUSON
RICHARD M. SAUNDERS

V·N·R Van Nostrand Reinhold
TORONTO   NEW YORK

A Van Nostrand Reinhold Book
Published by Fleet Publishers
A Division of International Thomson Limited
1410 Birchmount Road
Scarborough, Ontario, Canada   M1P 2E7

CANADIAN CATALOGUING IN PUBLICATION DATA

Ferguson, Mary, 1909-
    Canadian wildflowers through the seasons

Includes index.

ISBN 0-7706-0018-2 (bound).
ISBN 0-7706-0041-7 (pbk.)

1. Wild flowers — Canada.   I. Saunders, Richard
M., 1904-   II. Title.

QK201.F472   582.13'0971   C82-094709-1

DESIGN: Brant Cowie/Artplus
JACKET PHOTOGRAPH: Mary Ferguson
TYPESETTING: Compeer Typographic Services Limited
COLOR SEPARATIONS: Herzig Somerville Limited
PRINTING AND BINDING: McLaren, Morris and Todd Limited

Printed and bound in Canada
82 83 84 85 86 87 88 7 6 5 4 3 2 1

Contents

Introduction

FROM THE FIRST SONG of the robin until the last leaf falls, the lure of wildflowers takes possession of all who love them. It is a strange and powerful fascination that affects the naturalist and the photographer alike. Each in his or her own way prepares for the days spent seeking and photographing them.

To fall in love with wildflowers seems like a foolish thing to do, yet some people have spent their lives searching for them. They have endured all kinds of hardship and sometimes died in their quest. Peter Kalm, a student of Dr. Carl von Linné, usually known as Linnaeus, who lived from 1707 to 1778, journeyed widely throughout North America. He traveled north to Quebec in 1749 via Lake Champlain through warring Indian tribes, never able to sleep soundly for fear of being captured, until he reached Quebec. In his honor, the tiny Brook Lobelia he found was named *Lobelia kalmii*.

Wouldn't it have been wonderful to walk with John Macoun in 1872 across the prairies and see before you "an unbroken expanse of wildflowers" extending as far as the eye could see? Or to accompany Thomas Nuttall and John Bradbury about 1810 through a land of unspoiled beauty. Bradbury reported that they saw one place "full of innumerable clumps of wild rose and currant bushes, mixed with grape vines, all in flower and extremely fragrant. I have never seen a place equal to this in beauty."

But distance lends enchantment, and it wasn't all delight. These explorers in search of plants often trudged across vast distances on foot. They endured many hardships, from all kinds of insect bites, to attacks by grizzly bears and bouts with fever, far from help.

Thomas Nuttall was so overwhelmed by what he saw that he forgot where he was and became lost, nearly dying of hunger and thirst. Stalked by Indians and incapacitated by fever, he was later nicknamed *le fou*, "the madman," by the Canadian voyageurs whom he accompanied on part of one expedition to the northwest. Traveling by canoe was a real hazard because he couldn't swim, but he was not conscious of any danger. He used his gun barrel to dig up plants and to carry seeds. Needless to add, it was useless as a weapon of defense.

Another courageous botanist was David Douglas, a Scot by birth, sent to western North America by the Royal Horticultural Society of Britain. His second collecting trip began in 1825 at the mouth of the Columbia River. Going up the river, he found nearly 500 species of plants in six months. This was an exhausting trip during which he injured his knee. Among the seeds he sent to England were those of the tree subsequently named the Douglas Fir in his honor. After spending the winter at Fort Vancouver, where the rainy season had worsened his rheumatism, he started out again in spring, very eager to find another tree whose sweet, edible nuts had been given him by the Indian people. It grew in a difficult, mountainous region, a country of hostile Indians and grizzly bears. His eyesight became increasingly bad but he persisted, and finally in October 1826 he found the Western Sugar Pine. It is a very tall tree up to 200 feet (60 m), with the longest cones of any American conifer, 16 inches (41 cm) in length. They were at the very top and he had to shoot them down.

Those who now search for wildflowers do not face such hardships. Our aim is to photograph with all our skill the flowers that still remain in some places. Our desire is to show each subject to its best advantage in all its loveliness. The discovery of a rare or unusual flower, a new species we have not seen before, or an expanse of flowers in fields, woods or swamps exhilarates and spurs us on. We forget the swarming black flies and mosquitoes, the difficult progress into a bog or the tiring climb up a mountain trail weighted down with equipment. Into our pictures go all our love for these flowers, our joy at their color and structure, and all the skill we have acquired in years of practice. We take many pictures and spend many hours doing it. If even one or two photographs succeed in capturing the beauty we have seen, then we are rewarded for all our effort. If not, our resolve is to return next year and try again!

In this volume, we present 124 pictures of wildflowers or their seeds taken by 17 photographers, amateur and professional. We hope they will appeal to you. When you go out with the same purpose, take along patience and perseverance as part of your equipment, and take pictures for the joy of it.

Spring

IT IS JANUARY, and ice-laden cirrus clouds are sending their gracefully curling streamers, heralds of advancing snow, out across a sky of chilly blue. On the land below, powdery snow driven by westerly winds sweeps and swirls across hard-packed drifts in white, curling mimicry of the clouds above. In such a scene as this, the watcher wonders if the dream of spring will ever come true.

We should remember, however, that now that we have passed through the dark depths of the winter solstice, the sun has started upon its regular upward climb. The days are lengthening imperceptibly in the midst of blowing snow and glistening ice, yet to those who wait, the advancing seconds bear a message of promise and hope: the welcome tide of light and warmth has begun its annual northward flow.

The signs of springtime's genial approach mount as the sun teases hard and glassy icicles into dripping founts, or breaks open cracks in the snowy cover of silent streams to reveal the tumbling blue water beneath. South-facing banks become so warm they begin to shed their cloaks of snow. Along these warming slopes, perhaps in late February or early March, and often well before the snow has fully disappeared, shining pools and lanes of black ooze appear where springs now run free. In this friendly habitat, you may well expect to see what so frequently is the first flower of spring, the Skunk Cabbage, be it the multi-colored harlequin of the east or the golden beauty of the western coast. Now is the promise of spring, the emergence of fresh new life, beginning to be fulfilled.

For this great event, nature has long been wholly prepared. In plant and animal, in bird and insect, in all of nature's creatures breathes the anticipation that spring, the time of rebirth, will come again: witness the myriad waiting buds that rest on countless trees, shrubs and lesser plants. Formed and set last spring and summer amid those seasons' burgeoning green, humbly persistent through the outbreak of autumn's color panoply, and effectively protected against the assaults of winter winds and cold, these buds are to be counted among nature's forethoughts for the spring. These tight-decked little buds are pregnant with life, and as the warming breezes of spring caress them, that hidden life begins to stir.

From coast to coast along the mid-northern reaches of this continent, the Alders are among the first plants to respond to the gentle touch of spring. Their clusters of brown cones, last year's fruit, that have been so noticeable all winter long are nearly forgotten as our eyes are drawn to the elongating staminate catkins, those gold and brown mottled pendants that seem to laugh at the grey, retreating ice below. Beside the blue waters of some opening pond or rippling brook, the massed wands of Red Osier Dogwood, which have added lively reddish accents to a snowy world throughout the winter, gleam with burnished intensity. These stems and twigs announce in vivid red that spring has come and is sending stirring, invigorating sap coursing through them. What we read in red amongst the Osiers, we may see in yellow in the topmost branches of the Willows.

Freshening and strengthening color, however, is by no means the only way in which that welcome pronouncement, "The sap is running," is made. In these earliest days of spring, we have only to pass some sturdy Maple, be it in the countryside or along a city street, where recent winds have broken some branch or twig, and we will see crystalline pendants dangling from the breaks. These are no ordinary icicles, but rather "sapsicles" that are formed by the oozing sap of the Maple. Although it congealed as it first came out, sweet, gleaming globules of sap creep down the sapsicles now that the warmth of daytime has arrived.

In the realm of Maple, Beech, Oak, Aspen, Birch and all other deciduous trees, these are the days of the open woods. Here, light comes streaming down through the bare-branched, leafless trees, and with it comes warmth from the steadily mounting sun. Spring may seem to come in fits and starts, to hesitate and halt, as belated snowy winds whistle through the trees. Yet the day will duly arrive when upon entering the woods we discover that winter's white blanket has become torn, ragged and frayed. Openings are evident all around. Winter's last bastion drifts survive only on cold, north-facing slopes and in the black shadows of clustered evergreens and dark ravines. As warm-toned browning openings reach out amidst the tattered snow, more and more of a new-old carpet is revealed, the smooth, tan-colored, winter-pressed mat woven out of the leaves that fell last fall.

As we tread lightly across this leafy carpet that soon will have its nap raised by passing springtime breezes, we quickly find that nature has planted here the first of its seasonal gardens. Suddenly, in the midst of all the dead leaves, we spot a few emergent buds that are very much alive, green, tinged with brown-red and bronze. We have discovered a sheltered clump of Hepaticas, all cloaked in soft, grey silk, a protection from the cold of still-frosty nights and nearby snow. Looking on a little farther, we are rewarded with the sight of delicate white blooms, for some of their buds have opened. Then, all at once, snug against a sun-warmed tree trunk we discover an alluring cluster of these flowers, all wondrously coral pink. And only a hundred paces beyond, where a south-facing cliff plunges down to a woodland pond, we are brought to an abrupt halt by still another group of these blooms, this time decked in deep rich blue. Hepaticas commonly initiate the flowering in the open woods from their eastern edge along the Atlantic coast to their western fringes bordering the prairies.

As the tide of spring flows steadily northward, Hepatica blooms are quickly joined by those of other plants until the open woods are quite begemmed with flowers in all manner of colors and hues, from the mysterious smoky-blue of the Cohosh and the brick-red of the Wild Ginger, to the creamy-white sprays of Dutchman's Breeches and Squirrel Corn rising above spreading green mats of fragile, fern-like leaves. Soon, the company will include other, larger stretches of green above which will nod the yellow, recurved blossoms of the Common Trout Lily or, if we are fortunate, we may find the elegant, white flowers of its rarer relative, the White Trout Lily. So it will go from plant to plant, flower to flower, until the bare dark trunks of the woodland rise up above snowy banks of Great White Trilliums. Then, the garden of the woods will be at its peak of bloom.

In the meantime, along the damper verges of country roads, on stream banks and lake cliffs and in similar open wet places, the golden faces of the Coltsfoot will be turning upward toward the sun. Brought by the pioneers from their homelands over the sea, Coltsfoot was imported as a valued herbal medicine used in the treatment of colds and coughs. Like a great number of introduced plants, it has long since gone wild and become naturalized. It is now one of the earliest flowers of spring. Growing also in open wet spots along the borders of ponds, marshes and swamps, is our native Pussy Willow, which to so many people symbolizes the coming of spring. The furry, grey catkins, or "pussies," of this plant appear long before any leaves. The pussies are the warm protective covering of the developing flowers. When these come into bloom, they will coat their catkins with shining gold.

We may approach a bog some spring day as we descend a flower-studded woodland slope. A solid mass of dark Spruces, pyramidal Cedars and viridescent Tamaracks seems to bar our way, yet a gentle stream provides a gateway into the bog. Once through, we find that the bog, however dark and tangled it at first appears, is a region of subtle, changing lights. In the midst of gloom, a shaft of luminescence reveals a green and vital mound all flecked with white. We have discovered the creamy blossoms of the Goldthread, one of the earliest of bog flowers, but its secret will remain concealed until we probe beneath the green cover on the mound. Under this creep the thread-like golden rhizomes, once used as a source of yellow dye.

A secret thus revealed inspires us to look for others, and so we bend our meandering tracks from one light-touched gap to another, alongside glistening little pools, everywhere with an examining eye. In this way, we come to our second floral puzzle, a huddle of tiny plants seeming so bare and insignificant as hardly to warrant a second look. And yet when we focus on the minute flowers, we realize we are looking upon a master example of nature's artistry: the intricate green-gold fringed fretwork that are the petals of the Naked Mitrewort. The spring bog is clearly a land of wonder and mystery, inviting and rewarding investigation as it will throughout the entire flowering season.

As spring presses northward across the latitudes, its influence becomes evident everywhere, along the east and west coasts, through the open woods, into the hills and valleys, down into the bogs and across the prairies, stirring and greening the world. By mid-June, it will be nudging the Arctic and starting to climb the highest mountains. These last two regions are the final places to receive the touch of spring and they have much in common: cold and wind and long-lasting burdens of snow and ice.

Hence, you may tread the valley roadsides and trails near popular resorts in the Rockies in late June or early July, finding them rich with bloom, but as soon as you start to climb the mountain paths you will soon see snow ahead. And looking up some slope, you may be startled to see what looks like a yellow wave coursing down between the drifts toward you. This is no wave of water descending, but a vast array of Glacier Lilies marking on this slope the edge of spring.

Higher yet we go, coming soon to little green patches beside a tumbling brook whose overflow has cleared these spaces of bordering snow, where every space is dotted white and yellow with Globe Flowers and Snow Buttercups. Along the farther limits of the green, some of these same plants in bloom have their flowers collared in snow, zealously anticipating the spring. Finally, we are above the treeline and into solid snow. Surely there are no flowers here! Let us not be so certain, though. Look over there at that line of grey rock rising above the snow and facing to the south, reflecting the spring sun. A narrow space has been sliced off the snow by the warming rock, and in this slit stands a brave company of smiling pink faces, Bog Laurel, flanked by the white bells of Mountain Heather. At this height spring arrives late, but it always arrives, and the plants are ever ready to greet its advent.

By the time the spring has thrust its frontier high up on the mountains and is edging into the Arctic, it has created throughout the land a massive stirring of renewed life. A burgeoning of bloom and wave upon wave of grasses now clothe the prairies and adorn the open fields. Leaves have emerged on every tree and bush of the once bare deciduous woods. No trail marker of the seasons is more noticeable than this drawing of a green cover over those open woods that so early burst into bloom under the urging of the spring sun. In these latter days of spring, warmth is yet increasing, and throughout the woods a subdued green light now prevails. In this changed woodland setting, spring flowers are finishing their course. Henceforth the current of profuse bloom will follow the sun into the open spaces. Spring is giving way to a new season, to the luxuriance and bounty of summer.

Wild Lupine

Lupinus perennis

LEGUMINOSAE

Henry David Thoreau wrote that the Lupine paints a whole hillside with its blue, making such a field as Persephone, Greek goddess of flowers, might have wandered in. There are many species across North America in all colors, but the largest number have blue flowers. Since they grow in poor soil, it was believed years ago that they deplete the soil of all its nutrients. Thus, the plant was named Lupine, from *lupus*, the Latin for wolf. Actually, like all legumes, Lupine enriches the soil where it grows. In Texas, one species called "Bluebonnet" is the state flower.

The Wild Lupine grows to a height of 2 feet (60 cm). It blooms from April to July, from southern Ontario to Minnesota, and southward in the United States to Texas. Its attractive leaves are made up of seven to eleven leaflets arranged in a palm shape. These leaves seem to be somewhat light-sensitive during the day and partly fold their long fingers at night.

The famous Russell Lupine, developed by a Yorkshire gardener a number of years ago, grows wild in the Maritimes, where it covers roadsides and fields with its rainbow colors.

Harvest Lily, Fool's Onion

Brodiaea coronaria

LILIACEAE

In dry, gravelly places and on roadsides, this Lily blossoms from May to July, often against an unattractive background of dead grass and shriveled leaves. Its bright blue flowers can be seen from southern British Columbia to California, west of the Cascade and the Sierra ranges. The flowers form a loose cluster with stalks, or pedicels, of different lengths. Six tepals form a tube containing six stamens, three fertile with long anthers, and three white, petal-like sterile ones. The plant grows 4 to 16 inches (10 to 40 cm) tall.

The root is a rounded corm. In 1792, Archibald Menzies, a surgeon-botanist exploring with Captain George Vancouver in Puget Sound, reported that he saw Indian women digging up the bulb-like root of this Lily. It formed a part of their subsistence diet, as did raspberry shoots and a kind of barnacle. Today, the plants are not plentiful enough to dig and need protection if they are to survive.

Brodiaea commemorates James Brodie, a Scottish botanist who died in 1824. *Coronaria* is a Latin adjective meaning "used for garlands." There are several other Brodiaea lilies in North America, the most beautiful of which is the scarlet Fire Cracker Flower, found in California.

Farewell-to-Spring

Clarkia amoena
(syn. *Godetia amoena*)

ONAGRACEAE

In the 1860s Spanish children in southern California called it *Adiós primavera*, or just *Adiós*, so now in English it is called "Farewell to Spring," a rather sad name for a charming flower. "Summer's Darling", another common name, seems more suitable, especially since the former name is often given to two other species of *Clarkia*.

The genus name, *Clarkia*, was given in honor of Captain William Clark of the Lewis and Clark expedition of 1804 to 1806. These men were the first people of European extraction to cross the Rocky Mountains to the Pacific.

The leaves are long, narrow and alternate. The flowers, which appear from June to September, have four fan-shaped petals that vary in their color and in the size of their crimson markings. The height of the plant may be from 3 to 30 inches (7 to 76 cm). Blooming in open or wooded dry and grassy areas, from south Vancouver Island to California west of the Cascades, it is most common in central California where it borders some roadsides.

The seeds of Summer's Darling may be collected in September and planted in a suitable part of the garden. They will do well, provided they are not disturbed. Several hybrids have long been popular in English gardens.

Striped Coralroot

Corallorhiza striata

ORCHIDACEAE

The rosy-red flowers of Striped Coralroot, so brilliant on a sunny day, may be hidden in the forest shadow when it is overcast. This is the largest and most beautiful of the Coralroots of North America, reaching 6 to 20 inches (15 to 51 cm) in height. Its habitat is rich, moist woods in areas with alkaline soil, from British Columbia to Quebec, and south in the mountains to Mexico.

The plants are saprophytic, taking their food from dead plant material underground, and have no green coloring.

Corallorhiza is from the Greek words *korallion*, coral, and *rhiza*, root. This describes the coral-like form of the underground rhizome. *Striata* is from the Latin *striatus*, meaning "striped," and refers to the floral parts.

Canada Violet

Viola canadensis

VIOLACEAE

Letters by Canadian pioneer Catherine Parr Trail written in 1836 described the violets she saw as of every color, but without the fragrance of the Sweet English Violet. Over one hundred years later, it is still possible to delight in many species of Violet, of which Canada Violet is one of the more common. Found in bloom from April to July in rich deciduous woods, its white petals, tinted purple on the back, are among the loveliest of spring flowers.

Its range is from Quebec to Montana and south to Utah and Alabama. This is one of the stemmed Violets, meaning that the leaves and flowers develop from a stem which grows up from the rhizome or root. It may attain a height of 15 inches (38 cm).

Violets have been celebrated in song and story for centuries, and were said to symbolize modesty, chastity and loyalty. For that reason, they were always included in a bride's bouquet. Old herbals tell how important violets were in flower cookery: the leaves can be eaten raw in salads, fried in butter, chopped for an omelette or put in consommé. The flowers can be added to jellies and liqueurs, coated with a sugar syrup for use in sherbet, or with egg white and sugar and used as decorations on cakes and desserts.

Nodding Trillium

Trillium cernuum

LILIACEAE

Modest would seem to be an appropriate description of this most northerly distributed of the Trilliums. Its nodding or pendant bloom, hanging below a whorl of three broad leaves, is at first glance almost hidden from view. Yet, when discovered, its white or pink-tinged trio of inch-long (2 cm) petals, recurved very like those of a Turk's-cap Lily, make as signal an impression on the viewer as any neighboring flower. Later in the season, its six-angled, red-purple berry is equally worthy of attention. Careful hunting may be necessary to find this Trillium, for though it grows from 5 inches to 2 feet (13 to 60 cm) high, it may be well concealed in the midst of masses of other green plants.

The Nodding Trillium blooms in damp, acid bogs and wet woodlands from April to July. Its range is from the Mackenzie Valley to Nova Scotia to Newfoundland and south to Iowa, Tennessee and Georgia.

Bogbean, Buckbean

Menyanthes trifoliata

GENTIANACEAE

In the smooth backwater of a stream, in a sheltered corner of a small lake or in a bog, the white clusters of Bogbean barely rise above the surface. Each star-like flower has five white petals joined at the base to form a tube. Each petal appears to have collected shreds of white filaments on its upper surface. The anthers are black and gold, and the pistil is green. There may be ten to twenty flowers along each stalk, including some pink-tipped buds at the top, flanked by large, three-part leaves.

Theophrastus, the early Greek botanist, named the genus *Menyanthes*, combining two Greek words, *menyein*, disclosing, and *anthos*, a flower. Perhaps this describes the successive opening of the flowers from bottom to top. *Trifoliata* means three-leaved. The plant grows across North America from Alaska to Labrador, and south to the central part of the United States. It blooms in May and June, rising to a height of 4 to 12 inches (10 to 30 cm).

This plant also occurs in northern Europe and Asia. In Sweden, it is used as a substitute for hops in the making of ale; in Lapland, the roots are cooked as a vegetable.

Ninebark

Physocarpus opulifolius

ROSACEAE

Like bridesmaids' bouquets ready for the wedding ceremony hang the rounded clusters of white blooms upon the Ninebark bushes, from May to July. A new stage of loveliness appears for this plant in the fall when reddish seed capsules decorate the bushes. Its beautiful flowers and attractive fruit have made this plant a widely cultivated favorite. The bushes grow from 3 to 10 feet (1 to 3 m) high. Their common name is earned because of their peeling and shredding bark. The dark green, three-lobed leaves resemble those of the Highbush Cranberry as the specific name, *opulifolius*, indicates. Ninebark is one of the most striking floral ornaments of rocky stream banks and lakeshores.

The species grows from Minnesota to Ontario and Quebec, and south to Tennessee and South Carolina.

Small Round-leaved Orchis

Orchis rotundifolia
(syn. *Amerorchis rotundifolia*)

ORCHIDACEAE

In moist, lime-rich swamps and woods, this lovely flower blooms in June and early July. Rare in the east, it is more common in the north and west, from Alaska to Newfoundland, south to British Columbia and Montana, and east to New England.

The generic name, *Orchis*, was used by Theophrastus to describe the shape of the thick, tuberous root of the many European species. *Rotundifolia*, meaning round-leaved, describes the single leaf at the base of the flower stalk, or raceme, which grows 6 to 10 inches (15 to 25 cm) tall. There are from two to fifteen small flowers on each raceme. The petals are white or pale pink with a prominent spotted lip. Occasionally, the lip is striped. A curved spur can be seen extending from the orifice at the center below the column.

The small, delicate blooms of this plant, also called the One-leaf Orchis, may be enjoyed in western parks. Since the roots are delicately attached to moss or humus and are easily broken, the flowers should not be picked. Like most orchids, it does not transplant.

Black Lily

Fritillaria camschatcensis

LILIACEAE

The rich, dark brown of the bell-like flowers looks black in the shade, giving Black Lily one of its common names. The other English names — Eskimo Potato, Northern Rice Root and Indian Rice — refer to the fairly large white bulb, which has small offset bulblets that look like grains of rice. These bulbs were dug and eaten by all the coastal Indians, but are bitter and no longer popular as food.

The plant was named by the Swedish botanist, Linnaeus, in the eighteenth century. *Fritillaria* is derived from the Latin *fritillus*, meaning a dice-box, probably referring to the shape of the seed capsule. *Camschatcensis* likely refers to the plant's northern range, since Kamchatka is in northeastern Russia. These lilies may be found from Alaska to Washington near the Pacific coast. They thrive in open spaces, often near the shore where their roots can reach water.

This species of Fritillary is a shorter plant than *Fritillaria lanceolata*, which is also called Rice Root. Growing 12 to 18 inches (30 to 45 cm) tall, its flower arrangement is more compact, its petals are less mottled, and it has an unwinged seedpod.

Coastal Strawberry

Fragaria chiloensis

ROSACEAE

It is said that a sailor never wants to live far from the sea. This is also true of Coastal Strawberry, which is found close to the Pacific Ocean from Alaska south to Chile, and on the shores of Hawaii. The plant is low growing, clinging to rocky headlands and sand dunes. Its leaves are dark green and glossy with three leaflets on a long red stalk. The flowers, blooming from April to August, have five white petals. The strawberries ripen from June to August, depending on location. They are large for wild berries, usually a half inch (1 cm) in diameter, and fragrant. It was their delightful perfume that gave the genus name, *Fragaria*, from the Latin *fraga*, meaning fragrant. The species name tells of one of its homes, the island of Chiloé, off the coast of Chile.

The English name, Strawberry, comes from the old Anglo-Saxon, referring to the plants' long runners, which are "strewed" all over the sand or rock. These runners are often abundant, and help to anchor the shifting sands of the beach.

In the late eighteenth century, *Fragaria chiloensis* was crossed with other species, including *Fragaria virginiana* (page 43), resulting in a large strawberry which could be grown commercially.

Naked Broomrape,
One-flowered Cancer-Root

Orobanche uniflora

OROBANCHACEAE

Naked Broomrape is a parasitic plant. With no green chlorophyll in its leaves or stems, the plant cannot manufacture food, so it attaches itself to the roots of a variety of trees and plants, including Stonecrops, (pages 31 and 61), and takes all its food from them. Growing in moist open places, the range of Naked Broomrape is from Alaska to Nova Scotia, and south as far as California, Texas and Florida. The flowers grow on top of a hairy and leafless stalk, 1 to 4 inches (2 to 10 cm) high, blooming from April to August. Usually white in eastern North America, the flowers are more often mauve to purple in the west.

Orobanche comes from two Greek words, *orobos* meaning vetch, and *anchein*, to strangle, referring to its parasitism. *Uniflora* means one-flowered, as this species is. There are several species of Broomrape in Europe and North America with more than one flower on each stem.

Common Cat-tail

Typha latifolia

TYPHACEAE

These familiar plants form a large part of the vegetation in our marshes. They also grow in wet places beside streams, on lakeshores, and in roadside ditches. In early spring, Red-winged Blackbirds sing their mating songs perched on the cat-tails and build their nests among the dead leaves and cat-tails of the previous year.

These plants grow to a height of 3 to 9 feet (1 to 2.7 m), with tall, sword-like leaves. They may be found from Alaska to Newfoundland and throughout most of the United States, blooming in late spring and early summer. At that time, the green, immature flower spikes may be gathered before they are released from their sheaths. These can be boiled and eaten like corn-on-the-cob. Pollen from the mature male flowers at the top may be used to extend flour in baking, and adds protein and a distinctive flavor to muffins. In very early spring, the creeping root stalks put out shoots which may be eaten raw, or cooked until tender in boiling water. These may store toxic substances, however, so be careful where you gather them. Cat-tails were an important source of food for some Indians, who also wove the dried leaves into mats, baskets and platters.

Typha means a bog and *latifolia*, broad-leaved. Another species, *Typha angustifolia,* is distinguished by narrower leaves and shorter, smaller cat-tails.

Field Horsetail, Common Horsetail

Equisetum arvense

EQUISETACEAE

The Horsetails are the only survivors of a group of plants that grew on the earth 250 million years ago. In those far-away times, some Horsetails were tree-size, but the existing twenty or so species are much smaller than their ancestors.

The Horsetails are common on roadsides and open low ground, from Alaska to Greenland and south throughout most of the United States. Reproduction takes place without true flowers, as it does in other such flowerless plants as ferns and mosses. From March to June, the brown fertile stems push up through the ground in great numbers. These fertile stems rise to a height of up to 12 inches (30 cm). On top of each is a cream-colored fruiting cone with brown spots, the sporangia, or spore casings. These hold the spores, which are released and under the right conditions grow into the small, green, lobed prothalliums. From these develop the sexual parts that unite to create new plants.

The fertile stalks wither away after the green, infertile ones appear. These green stalks are jointed and bear circular whorls of narrow green branches at each joint. Each branch matures to a length of 2 to 12 inches (5 to 30 cm). The plants are perennial, with a tough, slender underground root.

Small White Lady's Slipper

Cypripedium candidum

ORCHIDACEAE

This Slipper Orchid is listed as an endangered species in Ontario, Wisconsin and Illinois. It is regarded as rare in all parts of its range, from southern Ontario, west to North Dakota, east to New York and New Jersey, and south to Nebraska and Missouri. Its home in bogs and on wet prairies is often shared by the Yellow Lady's Slipper, with which it hybridizes. The habitat is usually lightly shaded by Tamarack, Red Osier Dogwood and Labrador Tea.

The botanical name describes the flower: *cypripedium* means slipper of Venus and *candidum*, shining white. Blooming in May and June, the slipper or pouch is egg-shaped and white with faint purple markings. Sepals and petals (except the slipper) are yellow-green. The leafy stalk is 6 to 16 inches (15 to 40 cm) in length.

If you are fortunate enough to know where this plant grows, admire its beauty and be careful not to disturb it. This orchid does not transplant and should never be picked.

White Trout Lily,
Fawn Lily

Erythronium albidum

LILIACEAE

The graceful flowers of this Lily appear on the floodplain of some streams and in rich moist woods from late April to early June, about two weeks later than those of its dainty cousin, the Yellow Trout Lily. Its bright golden anthers contrast with its white, recurved petals. The back of each petal is a faint purple color. A pair of long fleshy, faintly mottled leaves grows up from the ground, and the plant reaches 6 to 10 inches (15 to 25 cm) in height.

The deeply-buried bulbs or corms are attached to the leaves and flower stalk by a long, fragile root stalk. Picking the flower and leaves usually breaks this stalk, and the bulb withers and dies.

The genus name, *Erythronium*, dates from the time of Pliny the Elder, known for his encyclopedia of natural sciences. The word is from the Greek *erythros*, meaning red, referring to the pink petals of the single European species, *Erythronium dens-canis*. *Albidum* means white. There are fifteen or more North American species in this genus, most growing in the west.

Western Calypso, Deerhead Orchid

Calypso bulbosa (f. *occidentalis*)

ORCHIDACEAE

The woods are dense and dark with an occasional shaft of sunlight piercing the deep shade where Calypso makes its home. A single, nodding pink slipper sheltered by its crown of vivid tepals rises on a slender stalk above the single leaf. Only someone watching for it will see the May bloom of Calypso.

This small orchid was named for the sea nymph who lured Odysseus to her island, and kept him under her spell for seven years. It lives in cool woods, most often in an area with lime-rich soil. There are two varieties found from Alaska to Newfoundland, and south to California and northern New England. The western variant has similar petals and sepals of a deep pink, with white hairs on the lip of the slipper, growing 3 to 8 inches (7 to 20 cm) tall. The variety growing east of the Coastal range is pale pink with yellow hairs.

Archibald Menzies, a botanist travelling with the navigator, Captain George Vancouver, described it "in vast abundance about the roots of pine trees" near Port Discovery (now in Washington State) in May 1792.

Today, this orchid is rare, although a large number may grow together in a favorable location. Admire its beauty and fragrance, take its picture without disturbing it and leave it to enjoy its solitude in the woods.

Broad-leaved Stonecrop

Sedum spathulifolium

CRASSULACEAE

This Stonecrop's rosettes of thick leaves cling tightly to the rocks of the Pacific coast, often just above the tide line. Although this plant grows farther inland on rocks or on gravelly soil, it is most colorful when near the sea. The fleshy leaves are usually green with a white bloom in the spring, but at other times of the year may be rosy-red to lavender or purple. The flowers bloom from spring to late summer on long red stalks, which reach a height of 8 inches (20 cm). Sometimes, this plant is host to the parasitic Naked Broomrape (page 25) which grows throughout its range, from southern British Columbia to California, west of the Cascade Mountains, mostly on the coast.

Sedum means to sit, referring to the way these plants squat on rocks or gravel. *Spathulifolium* describes in Latin the thumb-shaped leaves which form the basal rosette. The young leaves of all Sedums are said to be edible, becoming bitter as they mature, but they should only be used in an emergency since this plant is becoming rare. Some species cause headaches if too much is eaten.

It would be an ideal rock garden plant if grown for that purpose by the nurseries, though it might only survive in the mild climate of the coast.

Yellow Sand Verbena

Abronia latifolia

NYCTAGINACEAE

From spring to late summer, this yellow flower ornaments coastal beaches and sand dunes. The stems supporting the erect flowers and leaves are often buried in the sand, so that they give no clue to their length, at times as much as 6 feet (2 m) in every direction. Sand adheres to the broad leaves and stems, which are covered with sticky hairs. The weight of the sand helps to keep the plant in place, as does a deep root system.

The yellow flowers are tubular, with five flaring lobes. They are joined into a round head on top of a 6-inch (15-cm) stalk. Very fragrant, their scent is like that of Heliotrope.

This plant was first reported by Archibald Menzies in 1792, when Captain George Vancouver's exploring expedition anchored off the California coast. More than twenty years later, Dr. Johann Eschscholtz, naturalist and surgeon accompanying the Russian expedition of 1816, collected and named it. The range of this hardy perennial is from British Columbia to southern California on the coast.

The generic name is from the Latin *abros*, meaning delicate, rather inappropriate for this species, but which may suit other members of the family. *Latifolia* means broad leaves.

Tall Mahonia, Oregon Grape

Berberis aquifolium

BERBERIDACEAE

In April and May, the many golden-yellow flower clusters of Mahonia shine in the sunlight above their dark green leaves. They have a wonderful perfume. This fine shrub grows on sunny slopes to a height of 3 to 6 feet (1 to 2 m), or taller in favorable locations. It is found throughout southern British Columbia, Washington, and Oregon, mostly west of the Cascade Mountains, and is the state flower of Oregon.

Berberis is from the Arabic meaning pointed leaves. The specific name is from the Latin *aqua*, meaning water, and *folium*, leaf. This describes the glossy, wet-looking leaves, which are composed of five to eleven pointed leaflets. Each leaflet has many spiny teeth, rather like a holly leaf. The berries ripen in August, and their color changes to a bright blue with a bloom. Then, the common name of Oregon Grape seems most appropriate. The berries taste like those of Wild Grape, and are sweetest after a frost. They yield a juice which makes a refreshing drink when sweetened; with the addition of pectin, this juice can be made into a jelly. Mahonia berries are a good source of Vitamin C, but are too acidic to eat raw. They should never be consumed in quantity, either raw or cooked, because they contain an alkaloid which may be toxic in large amounts.

Round-leaved Sundew (Leaf)

Drosera rotundifolia

DROSERACEAE

The pretty, red-tinged rosettes of Sundew leaves grow in sphagnum bogs and swamps. The filaments that extend out from each round leaf surface are tinted bright red and have sticky globules of fluid at the ends.

Only when Charles Darwin did experiments on the leaves was the true function of the red filaments explained. In his book about insectivorous plants, published in 1875, he explained that insects alighting on the central leaf surface are held fast by sticky globules of fluid. The longer filaments bend inward to help prevent the escape of the struggling insect. The larger the insect, the more filaments bend inward, until the whole leaf may be wrapped around a large insect. This can happen in less than a minute, but may take as long as forty-eight hours. The filaments are glands that secrete both the sticky, trapping fluid and the enzymes and acid required to digest the soft parts of the insect. When the prey has been fully digested, the leaves open and resume their former position, allowing the skeleton of the insect to blow away. In this way, the plant gets the nitrogen that its wet habitat does not provide.

The small white flowers bloom in July and August on stalks 4 to 9 inches (10 to 23 cm) high. They will only bloom in bright sunlight at mid-day, and open one at a time. Ironically, they are usually pollinated by the same kinds of small insects that are trapped by the leaves.

Yellow Monkey Flower, Common Monkey Flower
Mimulus guttatus

SCROPHULARIACEAE

This charming, bright-faced flower smiles at passers-by from the borders of streams, in bogs and seepage areas, and at the edges of lakes and rivers, from the mountains down to sea level. It grows in wet, sunny places from Alaska to Alberta and south to Mexico, and is occasionally seen in the east. The showy blooms appear from May to September. From 3 inches to 3 feet (7 to 90 cm) high, the plant sprawls over or rises above its moist home. It may be an annual or a perennial, and is variable in the shape of its leaves, in the size of its flowers and in the number of red spots on the lower lips.

Mimulus means little mimic, and *guttatus* means spotted. How suitable these names are, since the flat front of the flower with its open throat looks rather like a grinning face with freckles on it. If the throat is pinched, the mouth opens in what seems like hilarious laughter.

Other species vary in color from yellow to orange and red, with the greatest number of them being in California. Two other wide-ranging species, *Mimulus alsinoides* and *Mimulus moschatus*, are smaller plants. Their smaller, yellow flowers have few, if any spots.

Red-flowered Gooseberry, Gummy Gooseberry

Ribes lobbii

GROSSULARIACEAE

The Gooseberry's beautiful flowers hang down like small Fuschias below the branches. Thorns grow only at the nodes, and the small leaves are sticky on both surfaces, giving the shrub another common name, Gummy Gooseberry. Reaching a height of 3 to 5 feet (1 to 1.5 m) it blooms from mid-April to June and would make a fine garden shrub.

The hairy fruit ripens in summer and is edible. Opinion varies on its flavor; one source recommends it when fully ripe, while another calls it unpalatable. Found mostly on the west side of the Cascade Mountains from British Columbia to California, it is not common. Look for it in logged areas and on open mountain slopes. It roots easily from cuttings taken in spring or fall.

Ribes, the genus name for currants and gooseberries, is said to come from an old Arabic name for acid fruit. *Lobbii* commemorates William Lobb, an early collector of plants in California, where the species was first discovered.

Sea Blush

Plectritus congesta

VALERIANACEAE

In spring along the west coast, masses of Sea Blush tint the rocks pink. Inland, there are open, rocky places in the woodlands where Sea Blush and Blue Camas combine to produce an unforgettable scene. Blue-eyed Mary is another favorite companion. The range of Sea Blush is from southern British Columbia to California, as far east as the Cascade Mountains. The plants are annuals, growing on wet slopes and in meadows that are wet in the spring. The round head of tightly-packed flowers is at the top of the stem that grows 6 to 18 inches (15 to 46 cm) high, with a few small groups sometimes growing on the lower stalk.

The rather succulent leaves are smooth and opposite on an erect, square stem. They are oblong and entire. The petals join to form a small, flaring tube with five divisions at the mouth. The Greek word *plektos*, meaning plaited, is the origin of the generic name, and *congesta*, the specific name, seems to repeat the suggestion of closely-packed flowers.

In 1792, botanist Archibald Menzies, traveling with the explorer Captain George Vancouver, landed on Protection Island in the Straits of Juan de Fuca. He described the thick patches of Sea Blush growing just beyond the beach as the most delightful among wildflowers.

Dune Willow

Salix laurentiana (f. *glaucophylla*)

SALICACEAE

The photograph is of the male flower. These shrubs have some of the earliest flowers in the spring, blooming from March to May, before their leaves develop. Each plant has only one kind of flower, male or female.

The male flowers push out from the bud sheath to become a short, hairy catkin. This soft, grey catkin is often nicknamed Pussy Willow. As it matures, the stamens lengthen and change the color of the catkin to bright yellow. The female flowers, green at maturity, develop on another shrub. By the time the female flowers have developed, the leaves have burst out and the shrub is covered with green. The young Willow shoots were used by the Indians to make baskets, while the inner bark of some varieties was made into thread and used for fish nets.

The Willow family is large in the northern hemisphere. It includes tiny arctic trees that barely reach above the ground, a large number of shrubs and some tall trees. There are many introduced species, of which the best known is the Weeping Willow, *Salix babylonica.* Willows grow best near water. The range for the Dune Willow is Ontario, Quebec, Newfoundland and New Brunswick, south to Illinois, Ohio and Maine.

Goldthread, Canker Root

Coptis trifolia ssp. *groenlandica*

RANUNCULACEAE

Sheltered by the roots of a tree, small white flowers shine out like stars in the shadowed woodland. All around the flowers, shiny, dark-green, three-parted leaves form a fitting background. This is Goldthread, so called because its roots are thread-like and colored golden-yellow. The evergreen leaves last most of the year, with new leaves appearing around flowering time, May to July. The flowers grow above the leaves on stalks 3 to 6 inches (8 to 15 cm) high. *Coptis* is from a Greek word meaning to cut, alluding to the deeply divided leaves. *Trifolia* means three leaves, and *groenlandica* means from Greenland.

An inhabitant of mossy coniferous woods and swamps, Goldthread may be found from the Yukon to Greenland and Newfoundland, from southern Alberta to Nova Scotia and in the mountains to Tennessee and North Carolina.

The roots were used by many tribes of Indians to prepare a remedy for sore eyes. Early colonists learned about it from the Indians, and for many years the roots were collected for sale in the autumn. Goldthread roots were in constant demand and were listed in *American Medicinal Plants of Commercial Importance* up to 1930.

Common Butterwort

Pinguicula vulgaris

LENTIBULARIACEAE

The yellow-green leaves of the insectivorous Butterwort exude a sticky secretion from surface glands. Growing in a flat rosette, the leaves are oblong and about half as wide as they are long. Some may be up to 6 inches (15 cm) long in summer. The leaf edges have the ability to curl inwards very slowly when a small insect alights on a leaf. It is not known just what lures the midges, gnats and other tiny flying or creeping insects to this trap, unless it is the leaf's bright color or faint fungoid scent.

The leaves both digest and absorb their victims. An insect landing on the leaf immediately sticks fast. As it struggles, a digestive fluid begins to pour out of other leaf glands, allowing the leaf to absorb the insect. It is thought that the curving of the leaf edges helps to prevent the loss of this fluid, and also prevents the insect from being freed by rain. The movement is not rapid enough to assist in trapping the victim. Enzymes and acid are combined in the fluid to rapidly consume the insect. In this way, the plant gets enough nitrogen to live in the bogs, wet soil or on the wet limestone that it prefers.

The violet-like flowers are held on 2- to 5-inch (5- to 13-cm) stalks. These long, spur-red flowers have five flaring lobes, two at the top and three wider ones at the bottom. They appear in spring or early summer, across the north from Alaska to Labrador, and south into the northern United States.

Yellow Lady's Slipper

Cypripedium calceolus

ORCHIDACEAE

This beautiful wildflower makes its home in shady woods, cool bogs, swamps and even along the roadside in the cracks of the limestone in Ontario's Bruce Peninsula. Known in Europe as well as across North America, it is widespread from British Columbia to Newfoundland, and throughout the northern United States.

The flower blooms from April to July. Its bright yellow pouch, backed by three sepals (two of which are united) and two petals is supported by a leafy green stem, 12 to 24 inches (30 to 60 cm) long. The sepals are long, narrow and twisted, varying in color from green to dark brown.

The large, yellow pouch acts like a trap. Insects can crawl into the opening at the top, but because its edge is curled inward, they cannot climb out from the same place. Instead, they must exit through one of the small openings at the back, next to the pollen-bearing stamens, and take away with them some pollen, to be carried to the next flower. Charles Darwin watched the insect action and decided that the parts of this orchid were arranged to make cross-fertilization almost certain. Until his observations, it had not been understood how Lady's Slippers were pollinated.

Wild Columbine

Aquilegia canadensis

RANUNCULACEAE

Every breeze makes the Columbine flower dance on the end of its thin stalk. The Wild Columbine is pollinated by Hummingbirds and long-tongued bees lured by the sweet nectar at the end of the flower's long, thin spur. This perennial plant loves rocky, wooded or open slopes in bright sun. Its range is from Saskatchewan to Newfoundland and south to Texas and Florida. It blooms from June to September, reaching a height of 40 inches (1 m).

The generic name is thought to be from the Latin for eagle, *aquila*, from a fancied resemblance of the long-spurred petals to an eagle's claws, and at one time the flower was suggested as the national floral emblem of the United States, because of this botanical link to the national bird. The common name, Columbine, is from the Latin for dove.

John Tradescant, gardener to King Charles I of England, was the first in Europe to grow the red Columbine from Virginia. Gardeners accustomed to the native European blue Columbine, *Aquilegia vulgaris*, were delighted with the new flower, which was soon crossed with the blue to create many hybrids. During Queen Victoria's reign, messages were often conveyed by the types of flowers in a posy. A red Columbine meant "anxious and trembling," a purple one meant "resolved to win," while any other color meant "folly." Victorian ladies must have been able to interpret such a message as they wished!

Wild Strawberry, Common Strawberry

Fragaria virginiana

ROSACEAE

How delightful to happen upon a meadow of ripe wild strawberries on a fine June or July day, when the scent of the fruit is strong because the sun has warmed the berries.

The five-petalled white flowers bloom from April to June. They grow several to the stalk at about the same height as the leaves, 1 to 6 inches (2 to 15 cm) above the ground. The leaves have three sharp-toothed leaflets.

Strawberries may be eaten fresh, or made into jam or jelly. The fresh or dried leaves make a pleasant tea which contains some Vitamin C. At one time, about fifty years ago, it was possible to buy baskets of wild strawberries from the Indians. Now, no one picks them to sell — you must do it yourself. In the late eighteenth century, this species was crossed with *Fragaria chiloensis* (page 24) to produce the familiar hybrid that we cultivate commercially. The result was a larger plant, with larger, easier-to-pick fruit; however, both the flavor and the perfume of the berries were diminished.

The wild plants thrive in open, sunny areas and spread by runners, as well as by seeds. From Alaska to Newfoundland, and south to California, Colorado, Tennessee and Georgia, the Common or Wild Strawberry produces a most delectable fruit.

Sweet Coltsfoot

Petasites palmatus

COMPOSITAE

One of the first flowers of spring, Sweet Coltsfoot often begins to bloom in March, when snow still lingers on the ground, and may still be blooming in late June. This striking plant grows in moist woods and swampy places from the Yukon to Newfoundland and south to California, Minnesota and Massachusetts. Described as palmate, or hand-shaped, the leaves become very large by midsummer, up to 1 foot (30 cm) in width, and grow on stalks as tall as 2 feet (60 cm). By this time, the staminate flowers that are illustrated will have withered, and the pistillate flowers will have developed into a fluffy, cotton-like seed head.

Petasites is from the Greek *petasos*, which means a hat with a broad brim, and *palmatus* describes the shape of the leaves.

Leslie Haskin records in his book, *Wild Flowers of the Pacific Coast*, that the Indians who lived inland and could not get salt from the sea used to dry and then burn the leaves and stems. The resulting ashes were used as a salt substitute.

Sharp-leaved Hepatica, Liverleaf

Hepatica acutiloba

RANUNCULACEAE

Before Hepatica blooms in March and April, the winter blanket of snow must melt and the soil warm. While the leaves of the deciduous trees are still in tight bud, providing no shade to the woodland, the blue, pink or white flowers poke through the brown leaves covering the ground. These flowers open only on sunny days when insects are active. Occasionally, a double Hepatica occurs. In the garden of the farmhouse in Hammerby, Sweden, once owned by Linnaeus, the father of modern botany, there is a large Hepatica plant with pink double flowers. Each one is like a tiny Chrysanthemum.

The name, Hepatica, comes from the Greek word for liver. Centuries ago, it was believed that God had indicated that this plant should be used to remedy liver ailments by shaping the leaves like the lobes of the liver. This was called the "doctrine of signatures." It is not edible, and today is not used medicinally.

Hepaticas can be grown from seed in the cool, shady garden, if they have sunshine in the springtime when they bloom. The seed should be planted early in loose, rich soil, and kept moist. They grow from 4 to 9 inches (10 to 23 cm) tall, and are found in the wild from Minnesota to Ontario, Quebec and western Maine and south to Missouri, Alabama and Georgia.

Moss Phlox, Moss Pink

Phlox subulata

POLEMONIACEAE

A spreading mat of this low plant can blanket large areas. The clusters of flowers occur in such numbers that the short, narrow leaves may not show.

The flowers can vary in color from deep pink through all shades of pink, and from mauve to white. The dark red marking around the mouth of the calyx tube is characteristic. This perennial, with a prostrate, semi-woody stem, prefers dry, sandy or gravelly soil and is often found under oak and pine trees. It grows up to 5 inches (12 cm) tall.

The name *Phlox* is from the Greek for flame, and *subulata* means awl-shaped, describing the leaves. Frequently cultivated, it is a favorite plant for rock gardens, where it blooms profusely in spring. The plant is native to eastern North America, but has escaped from cultivation and extended its range from Michigan to Quebec, and south to Tennessee and North Carolina.

Few-flowered Shooting Star

Dodecatheon pauciflorum
(pulchellum)

PRIMULACEAE

From sea level to mountain meadow, this delicate flower grows in Alaska and the Yukon to Manitoba, and south to California, Mexico and Texas. Shooting Stars bloom early, spreading their pink beauty across bogs and meadows.

The flower stalk may grow up to 2 feet (60 cm) above the erect basal leaves, and supports an umbel or cluster of one to twenty flowers. The five petals are thrust backwards from the tube formed by the stamens. This is a confusing and variable species with many varieties; the petals may range in color from white to pink-magenta and lavender, with a yellow base; the plant may be smooth or hairy; however, no one mistakes a Shooting Star for any other flower once it has been recognized. There are several species, mostly of western distribution.

Dodecatheon, meaning the twelve gods in Greek, was the ancient name for Primrose. It was given by the Swedish botanist, Linnaeus, to this New World genus of the Primrose family. When the plant was brought to Europe from America in 1873, it was called the American Cowslip. It has also been called Indian Chief. *Pauciflorum* means few-flowered, and the former name, *pulchellum*, means beautiful.

Summer

WHEN DOES SUMMER ARRIVE? It seems a simple question to be answered by saying the twenty-first of June or the longest day of sunlight. This is a convenient and meaningful astronomical measurement, but the plain truth is that for most of us, summer comes unannounced. We go steadily along week after week enjoying and reveling in the on-going surge of new life which is spring. We believe that we are still standing in spring when all at once we realize, somewhat surprised, that we are in fact knee deep in summer. How did this new season come upon us so unnoticed? Clearly, we have been too immersed in the joys of spring to read the signs of seasonal change.

Should we not, for instance, have been paying more heed to the great billowing white columns of cumulus clouds climbing into the blue sky over our heads? They ride atop rising currents of warm air and become more and more common as days lengthen and warmth increases. The first of them may appear before the end of May, certainly by early June, well before the astronomical start of summer. Yet what could be more characteristic of the long, pleasant days of summer than these puffy white clouds sailing serenely across the sky? Sometimes they darken and make one think of imminent thunder showers, also a familiar summer phenomenon to which they point. These clouds are pointers or indicators of the warm season that is coming in. Let us miss not the signs in the heavens. Summer is on the move.

The signs sent by the clouds in the sky are manifest and easily detected, but the signs to be read in the open woods are subtle, gradual and far more likely to escape attention. As we wander through the light, airy aisles of the spring woods, we seldom give thought to their steady greening and the consequent dimming of light in them. So intent are we upon the search for and the pleasure in finding new flowers and plants that we commonly fail to notice that the number and variety of flowers around us is dwindling, until finally it is difficult to find them in the now well-shadowed woods. Spreading green, dimming light and dwindling bloom all tell us that conditions have changed, that spring is over and summer is upon us.

For the most part, plants in flower will be scarce, hard to find, even non-existent in the darkened woods of summer. Where trees have been knocked down by wind or lightning, cleared away by fire or flood or other means, openings may be created in which plants get a chance to flower and set seed that they would not otherwise have. Generally, however, the successful flowering plants of the summer woods are shade tolerant, or in some way especially adapted to living under such conditions.

One such peculiarly adapted member of the summer woods flora is the Wild Leek. This member of the Lily family is best known as a spring plant, for it deploys its great mats of dark green leaves during those early days when Hepaticas and Trout Lilies are in bloom. Indeed, many people celebrate spring by gathering these leaves for use in pungent picnic salads and stews. But during the spring, no flowers rise among the leaves, which die down and disappear as shadow comes to the woods. It is likely to be July when you may be startled to see clusters of shining white flowers dotting the dark woods floor. No leaves are visible, and you must puzzle a moment, or dig up one of the bulbs that are at the base of these umbels before you realize that they are the blooms of the Wild Leek. Their leaves manufactured food for the bulb in the spring when lots of light was available, and then disappeared. The well-fed bulbs have now sent up their lovely flowers, and when these have been fertilized, shining black, berry-like fruit will be produced. Thus will the Leek have completed its life pattern in the woods.

Even more fully adapted to the requirements of plant life in the darkened summer woods are those curious plants that have no green chlorophyll component in their make-up and so have no need of sunlight to manufacture food. Sometimes we come upon a group of them that seems to stand like a company of solemn ghosts, nodding their heads in the forest gloom. This kind we call Indian Pipes or Ghost Plant. Another sort masquerades as fallen twigs, and we may have difficulty telling woodland debris and living plants apart as we scout beneath the trees for Beechdrops. More easily detected are the orange-tinted Squawroot or the richly pink-hued spires of Pinedrops. These plants and their relatives draw their sustenance either from decaying humus as saprophytes do, or are directly parasitic upon other plants, as are the Beechdrops on Beech roots. They add an element of eerie beauty to the summer woods.

We may still go to the woods in summer to seek beautiful or strange plants, but if it is great displays of flowers we wish to see, we must travel the open spaces of the countryside. There, the tide of bloom flows in the fields, the meadows and pastures and all the other open areas where sun and light exert their benevolent influences.

The multicolored tapestry of warm summer fields is woven out of an endless variety of hues and shades, though it is usually whites, yellows and reds that predominate. In that respect, the Daisies and Buttercups are typical. No less so are those fields where our eyes follow the white haze of Queen Anne's Lace, sometimes as far as we can see. Or we may gaze in wonder at some dry pasture where an orange-red carpet covers the whole area, a tribute to the lusty success of a onetime garden flower, the Tawny Hawkweed, first brought to this continent only a little over a hundred years ago. In some places it could be tall, yellow-crowned heads of Elecampane that we see topping the lush greens of an abandoned field. The mouldering remains of a log cabin at the field's edge may suggest how this plant, source of a prized herbal medicine to the early settlers, came to be here. In fact, over a large part of the continent, a high proportion of our summer field flowers are ones that have been brought or have come accidentally from abroad, and which now are fully naturalized and prospering. They found the fields made by the clearing of the original forests immensely to their liking and needs.

The flowers of the field blithely travel through, over and around fences and hedges. Perhaps colorful masses of Lupines adorn the roadside banks, lines of tall Sunflowers or patches of bright, purple-faced Gaillardias. In many places, the road will be pleasantly framed by long expanses of yellow or white Sweet Clover, plants able to take quick advantage of any newly cleared space. Serried ranks of erect, fuzzy-leaved, yellow-flowered Mulleins may stand along some roadside that was but a raw scraped bank a mere two years past. Yet another plant that is becoming a familiar member of the roadside flora is that yellow beauty, the Birdsfoot Trefoil, which has spread beyond the fodder field onto the roadsides. It is evident that for those who seek sights of summer plants, roadsides can be one of their most rewarding hunting grounds.

Equally worthy of attention are railway embankments on both active and abandoned lines. In many parts, railways have preserved stretches of native flora that have been destroyed elsewhere by intensive agriculture and other human activities. This is notably true on the western prairies. Railway embankments everywhere are also likely to be occupied by the plants that travel with man, the kinds that do so well along the roadsides and plants that have literally traveled by rail. Once they were seeds loaded unknowingly at some coastal port, prairie town or inland depot along with the crates and bags of a more legitimate cargo. They have been unloaded as unwittingly as they were put on, perhaps dropped off by the swaying of the train or the sweeping of a freight car. Those that find the new sites favorable will germinate, grow and become the surprises of a plant hunter's day.

They may be many or few. They are unpredictable, yet always thrilling and astonishing when found. Who would think, for instance, that those fragile-seeming plants with tiny blue blossoms that we may find nestling in the cinders along a track are Dwarf Snapdragons that came somehow from Europe and traveled up the line? Who would expect to see the reddish blooms of an Umbrellawort, whose original home was probably a western prairie, along the fill of an abandoned line in the east? Yet these and many other plant surprises are sprinkled along the summer railway line.

Flowering interest and profusion, however, are by no means confined to the drier habitats, and open, marshy ponds or quiet lakes and rivers may be covered with fragrant Water Lilies. The muddy verges at the water's edge can be as prolific in bloom as the open water. In midsummer, we might be brought to a halt beside some marsh wondering about a pungent minty odor that we smell. Looking down, we discover a mass of green growth punctuated by whorls of pale purple flowers and realize that we have wandered into a patch of Field Mint. A little further exploration may well reveal white flowers hiding in the green luxuriance, either the open-faced blossoms of Arrowheads, or the white, fringed balls of Bur-reeds. Though often quite common, such semi-secretive plants might easily be overlooked. No one could fail to notice, however, those lines and mats of brilliant lemon-yellow that sometimes fill wet roadside ditches or cover large areas of open wet marsh and bog. They belong to the Bladderworts, curious insectivorous plants with little traps on their underwater or underground leaves for the tiny insects that they find a convenient source of food. Even more noteworthy can be the tall, scarlet-flowering ranks of the Cardinal Lobelia that, as summer progresses, stand like red-coated guards protecting the approaches to the precious wet places that are so necessary to the lives of many plants and animals.

In all the profusion of flowers of countless shapes, hues and tones that deck the summer countryside, it is easy to forget that the most common and basic color of summer is green. Yet all the flowering plants we delight to see and study, save only their dependents, the parasites and saprophytes, are clothed in this color. It is the coloring matter of chlorophyll, the elemental working substance in all green plants. As such, it is fundamental to the lives of all the living things that depend upon green plants for existence. When we look out upon the green summer, we are looking at the plant world at work.

In its latter days, summer — lush, profuse and full of life — puts on yet one more great surge of bloom, when brigades of Goldenrods and Asters march across the fields, setting up prospects of imperial gold and purple. It seems then as if the empire of summer will go on forever. Nonetheless, let us not be deceived, for though no set date can be allotted to its going any more than to its advent, the signs of its passing are already at hand. It could be but the last days of August that in the midst of the green of the Sumac grove an arc of vivid red flashes. On that same day down by the edge of the marsh, we may find an all but denuded Elecampane upon which a single ash-grey leaf curls gracefully in its old age just below a bouton of fox-toned fluff. And a few days later when September has arrived, we could stand in awe before a Red Maple, strikingly impressive in a dress of mixed red and green. These leaves upon the turn signal unmistakably that the rich, luxuriant season of summer is about to give way, that it will soon be replaced by crisp autumn, the season of sunset colors.

White Cockle, White Campion

Silene pratensis (Silene alba, Lychnis alba)

CARYOPHYLLACEAE

A bold invader from Eurasia, this robust plant accents fields, roadsides, railway embankments and many familiar or waste places with its striking flowers. They are white, or occasionally pink, an inch (2 cm) or so across, with notched petals. Male and female flowers appear on different plants from May to September. The fruiting capsules are urn-shaped, crowned with spreading teeth and highly polished.

This plant, also called White Campion, has a number of close relatives, and could be easily confused with Sticky Cockle, often known as Night-flowering Catchfly (*Silene noctiflora*). Unlike the White Cockle, the Sticky Cockle has both sexes in one flower and a network of green veins on the calyx. Its upper plant parts are much stickier, and the leaves below the flowers are narrow and long in contrast to the broad leaves of the White Cockle. Curious superstitions are associated with our plant, one of which is that if you pick a flower, you will be struck by lightning!

White Cockle grows 2 to 4 feet (60 to 120 cm) high, with spreading branches. It is common from British Columbia to Newfoundland, south to California, Utah, Missouri and North Carolina.

Slender Ladies' Tresses

Spiranthes lacera var. *gracilis*

ORCHIDACEAE

Remarkable for its ephemeral grace, this little Orchid is very unusual in its choice of habitat. It prefers to live in dry, sandy or gravelly fields, in open woods and on grassy slopes, unlike most of its Orchid relations that incline to damp areas. Its tiny, tubular, white flowers ascend a virtually bare stem in a rythmic spiral, with each small bloom bearing a distinctive green stripe on its lip. This stripe is more yellow in the southern part of its range. It occurs from southern Ontario to Nova Scotia in Canada, and extends south to Texas and Florida. It usually flowers from June to October, and sometimes into November. The leaves grow in the form of a rosette at the base of the stem, and are usually withered and gone before blooming time. Plants may reach 20 inches (51 cm) in height, but always give an impression of petite beauty. They may appear together in tremendous abundance in any one area.

Shadbush, Juneberry, Saskatoon Berry

Amelanchier species

ROSACEAE

Seen like fountains of immaculate white, or arching up against a deep blue sky, Shadbushes seem the very essence of spring, the epitome of fresh, new life in a clean, new world. At this stage with the leaves scarcely half-grown and still folded up the narrow-petalled flowers dominate the scene. Most Shads are bushy in form, hence the common name of "Shad-bush" for the genus but a few species may reach tree form and size.

Hybridization is fairly common in this genus; consequently variability of plant details is to be expected. This applies to the fruits as well as to other parts of the plants. Normally reddish-purple in color, they have long been valued, especially those of the species known as Saskatoon Berry, by both Indians and European settlers, being used in pemmican, in jams and jellies and pies. However, some Shads produce dry, insipid fruit that is scarcely edible. This seems to depend upon the species and the growing conditions.

Shad wood is hard and tough and is valued for the making of tool handles and fishing rods and in cabinet work.

Look for blooms in rich, open woods, old bushy pastures and on second-growth slopes, March to June, from Alaska to Newfoundland, south to Oklahoma, Louisiana and Florida.

Meadow Beauty, Deergrass

Rhexia virginica

MELASTOMATACEAE

Coming upon a group of these plants in some wet, sandy or peaty area, perhaps at the edge of a bog or marsh or along a lakeshore, can be one of the delights of a summer's walk. Its eye-catching flowers with rich, pink petals and conspicuous out-thrusting yellow stamens remind us in their luxuriance that this is a noteworthy member of a vast family of plants (Melastomaceae) which is almost wholly tropical in distribution. *Rhexia* is the only genus in the family to reach into North America. There are several species in the southern States, however, this is the only species that extends into Canada. Hence, its position amongst flowers is comparable to that of the Ruby-throated Hummingbird among birds of the same area, for it too is a sole representative of an almost wholly tropical family. Our plant may grow as high as 2 feet (60 cm) and bear distinctive winged stems. Rare and local in southern Canada, it becomes increasingly profuse to the south.

Meadow Beauty blooms July to September, from southern Ontario and Nova Scotia to Louisiana and Florida, occurring on what is known as the coastal plain.

Bird Cherry, Pin Cherry, Fire Cherry

Prunus pensylvanica

ROSACEAE

How the birds must rejoice when a good season produces a tree laden with fruit, as this one is! They lose no time eating the ripe fruit, and chatter as if in glee all the time. These tiny cherries make a delicious jelly, if you can get them before the trees are stripped of fruit. You need at least two quarts (liters), as the cherries are small and have large pits for their size, but the jelly is worth the trouble.

In early spring, these small trees are covered with white blossoms growing one flower to a stalk, in a cluster. The bark is reddish-brown and shines like satin. There are many conspicuous horizontal lenticils in it.

The trees grow in open places, along fences, on stream banks and at the edge of woods, from British Columbia to Newfoundland and south to Colorado and Tennessee. They bloom from April to July and the cherries ripen in July and August. Several other species of Cherry grow wild across North America. All are good to eat, if you use only the flesh of the fruit. Since all members of the genus, *Prunus*, have poisonous leaves and fruit pits, these parts should not be eaten.

Black Twinberry,
Bracted Honeysuckle

Lonicera involucrata

CAPRIFOLIACEAE

A sturdy shrub of 3 to 6 feet (1 to 2 m), Black Twinberry blooms with pale yellow flowers from April to August. The range is from Alaska to Quebec, and south in the mountains to California and northern Mexico. Locally abundant, but otherwise not common, it prefers lime soil and cool, moist woods or thickets. The shiny black berries ripen in July and August, and are not edible. The large leaves are prominently veined.

In the daytime, butterflies and bumblebees are frequent visitors to the flowers, which have a faint, pleasant scent; at dusk, moths come for nectar. Unlike many Honeysuckles, this one does not climb on other plants. It is a stiff upright shrub which displays its twinberries to advantage.

Lonicera, the generic name, was given to honor Adam Lonitzer, a German herbalist of the sixteenth century. *Involucrata*, the specific name, draws attention to the large leaf-like involucre or whorl of bracts around both flowers and berries. Behind the black berries, the involucre is bright red purple.

Spotted Lady's Slipper

Cypripedium guttatum

ORCHIDACEAE

From between a pair of basal leaves, a slender stem holds up a single orchid flower which varies greatly in markings and color, especially on the pouch or slipper. The spots are irregular and sometimes bright magenta, as in the photograph, but in the variety that grows in parts of Alaska and in Asia, the spots are brownish. Sometimes, large colonies of these Orchids grow under poplar trees with few other plants among them. The plant's habit of growth is comparable to that of the Moccasin Flower, *Cypripedium acaule*, with two similar basal leaves but, unlike any other *Cypripedium*, Spotted Lady's Slipper has a globular lip with a large opening. The pouch is lined with hairs, and has overhanging edges, so insects are apt to slip into it. Because of the extended margin, they cannot get out except toward the back, where a ladder-like arrangement of hairs permits them to climb up, brushing past the pollen, and so carrying it to the next flower. Above the pouch is a large sepal, hanging over the opening as if to keep the rain out. Two narrow, spotted petals extend at the sides.

This is an interesting and unusual Lady's Slipper. Growing up to 10 inches (25 cm) in height, it blooms in June and July, and may be found in Alaska, the Northwest Territories and the Yukon in North America, and across Siberia in Asia.

Spreading Stonecrop

Sedum divergens

CRASSULACEAE

A low plant with a spreading habit of growth,
its yellow flowers brighten many rocky places
in the mountains. The small flowers bloom
at the top of stalks 2 to 5 inches (5 to 13 cm)
high, from July to September. The five petals
have sharply pointed tips like little stars and
open only in the bright sunshine. The small,
oval leaves look fat and round. They are
opposite and usually red-tinged when it is
dry and hot. The plants grow easily from
seed in a rock garden.

Sedum means to sit, referring to the way
many plants of this genus hug the rocks.
Divergens describes the arrangement of the
seed follicles, which point outwards. It is a
common plant in its range, from southern
British Columbia to Washington and as far
south as Mount Hood in the Coastal and
Cascade mountains.

Shrubby Beardtongue, Shrubby Penstemon

Penstemon fruticosus var. *scouleri*

SCROPHULARIACEAE

Occasionally, this spreading shrub covers a rocky slope in the mountains with lavender, deep pink or white flowers so profuse that the plant's leaves and branches may be almost hidden. Shrubby Beardtongue grows up to 16 inches (40 cm) high, with narrow, lanceolate, or lance-shaped, leaves and large, tubular flowers. The fifth stamen, as with all Penstemons, is sterile and bearded. Found on open sites from the foothills up to 10,000 feet (3 km) in the mountains, its range stretches from British Columbia to Alberta, south to Oregon and east to Montana and Wyoming.

Long-tongued insects, such as butterflies, are attracted to these flowers, for only a long tongue can reach their nectar. There are over 200 species of Penstemon, all native to North America, and most of them grow in the western region. While precise identification is sometimes very difficult, it is easy to find the fifth stamen and name the plant Penstemon.

Musk Mallow

Malva moschata

MALVACEAE

Introduced from Europe as a garden flower, it has become naturalized in North America. The range covers southern British Columbia, Manitoba, Ontario and Quebec to Newfoundland, and south to Tennessee and Delaware. It grows in fields, on roadsides and in old gardens, blooming from June to August.

The plant grows up to 28 inches (71 cm) high with many branches and soft, hairy leaves and stems. The flowers may be white, pale pink or deep rose, with five triangular petals. The many stamens unite to form a tube around the styles, which are part of the pistil. The leaves are deeply cleft. When crushed, the flowers and leaves give a musky perfume.

Young Mallow leaves have been used as a thickener for stews, or as a cooked green. The generic name comes from the Greek word *malache*, meaning soft, which refers to the downy parts of the plant. *Moschata*, meaning musky, refers to its scent.

Prairie Smoke,
Pink Plumes (Seeds)

Geum triflorum

ROSACEAE

In May or June, parts of the prairies are tinted pink by the massed flowers of Prairie Smoke. The petals are cream-colored, but are almost hidden by the five bractlets of deep pink. These flowers open only enough to admit insects, especially bees in search of nectar, for pollination. They nod together in the breeze from the top of a hairy, pink stem about 12 inches (30 cm) high.

Across the prairies and into the lower foothills, especially in areas with lime soil, the range of this plant is from British Columbia to southern Ontario and south to California, Nebraska and Illinois.

Each common name describes one stage in the plant's growth: after blooming, the stems lengthen and the petals fall, allowing the pink plumes to develop; as the seeds ripen, the color fades and the seed heads turn pale grey, creating the illusion of smoke with every breeze; as the seeds are carried away by the wind, the plump plumes become thin, like an Old Man's Whiskers, another common name for this plant. It is also called Three-flowered Avens.

The name, *Geum*, dates back to the time of Pliny the Elder (AD 23–79). It was first given to a European species, *Geum urbanum*. *Triflorum* describes the three flowers joined in a group at the top of each stalk.

Pinesap

Hypopitys monotropa

PYROLACEAE

As its name implies, the best place to look for this interesting saprophyte is in a pine woods. Growing 4 to 16 inches (10 to 40 cm) high, this summer woodland plant resembles the Indian Pipe, a near relative. Unlike that plant, however, it has several nodding heads which are yellowish, tawny or red but not white, on each downy, bracted stem. These appear from June to October. As with the Indian Pipe, the heads turn down during blooming and become upright when fruiting has taken place. Pinesap is the rarer of these two species, but is more frequently seen in the west. Also called False Beech Drops or Many-flowered Indian Pipe, it grows in the humus of coniferous, especially pine woods, from British Columbia to Newfoundland, south to Mexico and Florida.

Small Purple Gerardia

Gerardia purpurea var. *parviflora*

SCROPHULARIACEAE

Although often widely spaced, the graceful Gerardia may at times blanket its damp, open habitat. The relatively small flowers are most often pink or rose-purple, but white blooms may sometimes occur in large numbers. The flowers are tubular to start, but flare into five-lobed, open-faced tops that are wide enough, if seen face on, to hide the tubular beginning. Plants vary in height from 4 inches to 3 feet (10 to 90 cm). The very narrow, pointed leaves grow in pairs, or sometimes in tufts, on four-angled stems.

Flowering in August and September, the plant flourishes in damp, open ground, in open bogs, along damp shores and in low-lying ground from Manitoba to New Brunswick and south to Iowa, Indiana, Ohio and New Jersey.

Common Dayflower

Commelina communis

COMMELINACEAE

This reclining plant has become naturalized in North America from its native Asia, and can be found on roadsides and in waste places in Ontario and Quebec and the eastern United States, growing 18 to 36 inches (46 to 90 cm) tall. The flower is small, with three petals. Two are blue and conspicuous; the third is tiny and white, and may be nonexistent. It blooms from June to October, each flower lasting only until noon of one day. The plant is fleshy, with spear-shaped to oval leaves that are considered edible. They may be used in salads, or boiled and served as a vegetable.

The genus name, *Commelina*, was chosen by Linnaeus, the Swedish botanist, to commemorate the three Commelin brothers, two of whom were famous botanists. They are represented by the two larger blue petals at the top. The third brother lacked energy and ambition, and suffering from poor health, died young, without publishing anything. He is represented by the small white bottom petal, which may be lacking in some flowers. Fortunately, he died before Linnaeus published the name in his book *Species Plantarum*.

Evening Star

Mentzelia decapetala

LOASACEAE

Called Evening Star because the large flower opens only after sunset, it is a beautiful sight at dusk. The pale yellow color can be seen by the moths who visit it and pollinate the flowers. The ten pointed petals are 2 to 3 inches (5 to 8 cm) long, with about 200 stamens in the center. These flowers grow singly at the ends of branches and bloom from July to September. The leaves are cleft and lance-shaped. All the foliage of the plant is rough and sticky with minute, barbed hairs, which cause the leaves to stick tightly to whatever touches them. This spectacular biennial grows on dry hillsides and low mountain plains east of the Rockies from southern British Columbia to Manitoba, and south to Nevada, Texas and Mexico.

Mentzelia commemorates C. Mentzel, an early German botanist. *Decapetala*, meaning ten petals, describes this species only. The usual number for other species is five.

White Avalanche Lily

Erythronium montanum

LILIACEAE

Growing only in alpine and subalpine meadows above 3,000 feet (900 m), this Lily comes up as soon as the snow melts, often carpeting the meadows with flowers. It can be seen in late July and August by the thousands on the southern mountains of Vancouver Island north of Port Renfrew, and in the Olympic and Cascade mountains. Its range is from southern British Columbia to northern Oregon.

The white flowers, centered with golden-yellow, are large, about 2.5 inches (6 cm) wide. In rain or fog, the Lilies droop and half close, opening wide and straightening their stems when the sun shines. The stalks may be a foot (30 cm) tall, with as many as six flowers to one stalk. The two basal leaves are not mottled, as are those of several other members of this genus. Like all Lilies, Avalanche Lilies have three petals and three sepals, all alike. The root is a deep corm that nestles far below the roots of meadow grasses and many other flowers.

Green Coneflower, Cut-leaved Coneflower

Rudbeckia laciniata

COMPOSITAE

Whether standing in great clumps along some river bank, or marching in line beside a wet roadside ditch, the Green Coneflower is a striking summer flower. The common name refers to its greenish-yellow central mound or cone where the modest disc florets grow. This cone elongates considerably in fruit. It is the bright yellow ray florets, reflexed in bloom, that call attention to this tall, graceful plant, which grows 2 to 10 feet (60 cm to 3 m) high. Most of the leaves, except the uppermost, are deeply cut, hence the species name, *laciniata*, and its other common name, Cut-leaved Coneflower. By emphasizing the ray florets and so creating full-flowering heads, horticulturists have produced the much beloved garden flower, Golden Glow. This garden form is now going wild on its own.

Green Coneflower blooms July to September, in wet places from Montana to Manitoba to Quebec, south to Arizona, Texas, Louisiana and Florida.

Common Sunflower

Helianthus annuus

COMPOSITAE

Common Sunflower grows wild all across the central area of North America, in open, sunny places. The flower heads follow the sun around from east to west every day. For many years, the Indians harvested the wild crop, using the seeds to make flour for flat bread, and extracting oil for their bodies and hair.

When explorers Lewis and Clark crossed the prairies in 1803, they wrote about the bright Sunflowers wherever they went. The plants were still plentiful in 1872 when John Macoun, the Canadian botanist, saw "one unbroken mass of tall flowering plants, twelve miles wide." He identified them as Asters, Goldenrod, Penstemons, and Sunflowers. How lovely such a prairie scene would be! Even today, when the prairies are used to grow grain, Sunflowers persist on roadsides and along fences, adding bright color to the wide open landscape.

Helianthus is a large genus of many species. *Helianthus annuus* is the wild ancestor of the cultivated Sunflower, whose larger seeds are roasted or used for oil or margarine. The generic name comes from two Greek words meaning sun and flower. This annual grows from 2 to 13 feet (60 cm to 4 m), and blooms from June to September. It is the state flower of Kansas.

Common Indian Paintbrush

Castilleja miniata

SCROPHULARIACEAE

One of the commonest of the 200 species of Paintbrush in western North America, *Castilleja miniata* grows in meadows and on slopes at medium and lower elevations in the mountains. It occurs in all provinces and states from Alaska south to California, Arizona and New Mexico. The tubular calyx is green and almost hidden. The vivid red or crimson bracts surrounding this central calyx are most conspicuous. The plants have a woody base and narrow lanceolate, or spear-shaped, leaves with few hairs. The species is quite variable.

All species of *Castilleja* are semi-parasitic. They fasten to the roots of grasses and other nearby plants and take part of their food from them.

The generic name commemorates an eighteenth-century Spanish botanist, Don Domingo Castilleja. *Miniata* comes from minium, the scarlet-red oxide of lead. The common English name is said to come from a legend about an Indian maiden who fell in love with a prisoner of her tribe sentenced to die by torture. She fled with him, but became homesick after awhile and stole back to see her people. Hidden from sight in the bushes, knowing she could not reveal herself and live, she cut her foot, and with the blood drew on bark a picture of the beloved valley. Where her blood fell on the ground grew the little plant with a scarlet brush-like top.

Wild Begonia (Fruit)

Rumex venosus

POLYGONACEAE

Belonging to a large family commonly called Sour Docks, this species has won a nicer name, Wild Begonia, because of its lovely, pink-winged fruits, which look like the flowers of a Begonia. There is no relationship between Docks and Begonias.

All species of *Rumex* can be toxic if eaten in quantity. They are common on the sandy parts of the prairies, and pose a threat to livestock. The plant grows from Washington to Alberta, across to Manitoba, south to California, New Mexico and Nebraska, and has recently spread into Wisconsin. In 1886, it was reported by botanist John Macoun as far north as Prince Albert, Saskatchewan.

The stout stem, 8 to 24 inches (20 to 61 cm) in length, has thick, broad leaves on it. The flowers are small and crowded among leafy bracts. As the seeds mature, the sepals become bright pink or red, large and veined (hence, the species name, *venosus*). The plant blooms from April to June, with seeds maturing from May to August. The plant is also called Winged Dock or Wild Hydrangea.

Early Spanish settlers in the south extracted tannin from the roots to use in tanning hides.

Prairie Loosestrife

Steironema quadriflorum

PRIMULACEAE

Stiff and rigid, like toy soldiers presenting arms, stand the Prairie Loosestrife plants in many a damp, open meadow. Narrow, needle-like leaves point upwards from a four-angled stem. In their axils, usually near the top of the plant, 2 to 3 feet (60 to 90 cm) tall, are the open-faced yellow blossoms, an inch (2 cm) wide, with their sharp-pointed petals. This member of the Primrose family should be looked for in wet meadows, bogs and along lakeshores in calcareous, or lime-rich, areas, from Manitoba to Massachusetts, south to Missouri, Kentucky and Virginia.

King Devil,
Yellow Hawkweed

Hieracium pratense

COMPOSITAE

The fact that the Yellow Hawkweed is called King Devil and its close relative, the Orange Hawkweed, is also known as Devil's Paintbrush, plainly shows the widespread dislike of these aggressive weeds. Their cheerful, flamboyant beauty is evident to naturalists, their threat to crops and pastures to farmers. This Hawkweed, like its relative, has a dense covering of black, glandular hairs on its stems and on the bracts of the flower head. It grows from 1 to 3 feet (30 to 90 cm) high.

Introduced from Europe, it is thoroughly naturalized and spreading widely throughout the cultivated countryside. King Devil blooms in fields, pastures, along roadsides and in waste places, May to September, from Ontario to Nova Scotia, south to Tennessee and Georgia, and also in British Columbia.

Scarlet Globe Mallow

Sphaeralcea coccinea

MALVACEAE

When in bloom, the vivid color and the large size of the flowers on this small plant attract immediate attention. It often grows in large patches by the roadside, spreading by its long roots and prostrate stems. It may be seen on the dry prairies of southern British Columbia east to Manitoba and south to New Mexico, Arizona and Texas, blooming in June and July. The grey-green plants grow to a height of 8 inches (20 cm) with deeply-cut, hairy leaves, each with three to five lobes. The flowers are 1 inch (2 cm) in diameter, and vary in color from copper-red to vermilion. They bloom from the bottom to the top of the stalk.

The generic name comes from two Greek words, *sphaera*, meaning a globe or sphere, and *alcea*, the ancient name of this genus. These words seem to refer to the shape of the fruit, which is like a five-segmented wheel of cheese, according to Dr. Lewis Clark in *Wild Flowers of British Columbia*. The specific name means red.

Day-Lily

Hemerocallis fulva

LILIACEAE

Far from their native land in eastern Asia, these Lilies have found a new home in eastern North America. Growing well in almost any kind of soil, they escaped from the gardens of early settlers and are now well established along roadsides and in fields. Found from Ontario to New Brunswick and south to Missouri and Tennessee, they bloom from May to August, reaching 2 to 6 feet (60 cm to 1.8 m) in height.

The name, Day-Lily, means just that. The flowers open in the morning and close by sunset, blooming only once. *Hemerocallis*, the generic name, means beautiful for one day when translated from the Greek. *Fulva* is the Latin for tawny-orange, which describes the color of the flower.

For centuries in Asia and Europe, the buds, flowers and roots have been eaten, raw or cooked. They have long been a favorite vegetable in China and Japan. The early shoots can be added to salads; the flowers added to stews help to thicken them, like okra, while the crisp tubers, dug early, washed, peeled and boiled in salted water, taste like corn. The only problem is, you can't both eat and enjoy the plants, but its parts are worth tasting once.

Copper-flower, Copper Bush

Cladothamnus pyrolaeflorus

ERICACEAE

The unusual copper color and the long, curved pistil of the flower make Copper Bush easy to identify. The flowers are about 1 inch (2 cm) wide, with five petals. The plant is a deciduous shrub up to 7 feet (2 m) high. The leaves are very thin, elliptic in shape with a smooth margin, and are an unusual pale green. The plant grows in wet forests, at the edge of bogs and beside mountain streams near the Pacific coast, from southern Alaska through British Columbia to Oregon. It blooms in June and July.

A genus of only one species, the generic name *Cladothamnus* is from two Greek words meaning branch and bush. The specific name means flowered like a Pyrola, because the long curved pistil is characteristic of plants of that genus.

Where conditions are suitable, this would be an attractive shrub for the garden.

Rough-fruited Cinquefoil

Potentilla recta

ROSACEAE

The showy flowers of this Cinquefoil, sometimes an inch (2 cm) wide, brighten fields, pastures, roadsides and waste places from June to September, or until the frost. Bunched at the top of large, branching, leafy plants, often 2 feet (60 cm) or more tall, the flowers are usually a sulphur-yellow in hue, though occasionally of a deeper tone, and the petals are markedly notched. The compound leaves are digitate or hand-like in shape, commonly having five spreading leaflets, and sometimes as many as seven. The plant's upright character is noted in its species name, *recta*, which means erect.

Introduced from Europe, it is spreading rapidly and is listed as a formidable weed in many areas. Its range is from British Columbia to Newfoundland, south to Kansas, Arkansas, Tennessee and Virginia.

Black Knapweed

Centaurea nigra

COMPOSITAE

This is one of a group of plants whose flowers closely resemble each other. Most are roseate or purplish in color, but the one which has been welcomed into our gardens, Bachelor's Buttons, is blue. The Black Knapweed, sometimes called Spanish Buttons, may not have rayed florets; if it does, then it is a rose-purple cousin of the garden favorite.

All the Knapweeds have been introduced, deliberately or accidentally, from Europe. This species can be very aggressive and weedy; it grows in fields and in waste places, and there are spots where it lines roadbanks, apparently endlessly, with its blooms. A vigorous plant, it grows from 1 to 4 feet (30 to 120 cm) high, branching towards the top. Its lower leaves may be slightly toothed, but most leaves are lanceolate, or spear-shaped, and entire. The tightly-packed bracts under the flowers are straw-colored at the base, deep brown or blackish above, and beautifully fringed.

The flowers appear July to October in British Columbia and Washington, from Ontario to Newfoundland, and south to Michigan, Ohio and Virginia.

Purple Goat's Beard, Oyster Plant

Tragopogon porrifolius

COMPOSITAE

One of the strange English names for this plant is derived from its generic name, *Tragopogon*, made up from two Greek words meaning goat and beard. The second English name, Oyster Plant, comes from the taste of the root, which may be eaten raw or cooked. *Porrifolius*, the specific name, means leaves like those of leek. Cultivated and highly prized as a vegetable by people who live on the Mediterranean coast, it was brought by early settlers to North America, and has spread widely. It is common across most of central and western Canada in fields and waste places, and may be found throughout the United States.

The attractive flower heads are made up of many red-purple ray florets backed by longer green bracts. They open at dawn and close at noon, so that it is hard to locate the plant among grasses by afternoon. It blooms from April to August. The seed heads are large and globular, like enormous dandelion seed heads. The seeds sail away on large "parachutes," distributed by the wind.

Two related species with yellow flowers are found in North America, *Tragopogon pratensis* and *Tragopogon dubius*. All are biennial with edible roots. They reach a height of 2 to 3 feet (60 to 90 cm).

White-fringed Orchid, Plume of Navarre

Platanthera (Habenaria) blephariglottis

ORCHIDACEAE

Hunting the White-fringed Orchid may become a testing summer adventure, taking you through long reaches of wet woods and tangled groves of Tamarack and Spruce, before you emerge upon a bog that moves beneath your feet. Still, the reward is great, for you will have entered one of nature's secret gardens, where colorful Pitcher Plants, Bog Rosemary, Rose Pogonia and other Orchids, especially the exquisite, snowy-white beauty that you seek, call for your attention. The plant, a foot (30 cm) or so high, is adorned with long-spurred, fringed blooms that seem like summer-defying snowflakes. These Orchids are becoming rare, but occasionally grow together in great numbers.

The plant blooms from June to October in open sphagum bogs, cranberry reaches, and acid, sandy swamp areas, from Michigan and Ontario east to Newfoundland, and south to Texas and Florida.

Partridge Foot

Luetkea pectinata

ROSACEAE

Forming dense mats of dark evergreen leaves and red-brown stems, this spreading plant helps to hold the soil against the onslaught of wind, snow and ice in the alpine zone. The trailing stems are woody, and the toothed leaves are deeply divided. The flowers grow in a compact cluster on top of an erect stalk rising 4 to 6 inches (10 to 15 cm) above the spreading stems. They have five petals, five sepals, many stamens and a five-lobed pistil. The time of bloom is from June to August.

The generic name is in honor of Count Lütke, a famous Russian sea captain, who sailed around the world in the early part of the nineteenth century. *Pectinata* means like a comb, referring, possibly, to the deeply-toothed leaves.

The name Partridge Foot was chosen because of the fan-shaped and cut leaves, which were fancied to resemble the foot of a partridge. It grows from high alpine to subalpine levels in moist places, ranging from Alaska and the Yukon to northern California, and east in the mountains of Alberta, Idaho and Montana.

Beebalm, Oswego tea

Monarda didyma

LABIATAE

Beebalm ranks high with gardeners because it is a favorite flower of Hummingbirds. Its glowing red color and pleasant perfume also recommend it.

The name, Oswego tea, was given by John Bartram, the Quaker botanist of Philadelphia. He found it in the eighteenth century at Fort Oswego, now in New York State, when he was sent to arrange a peace treaty with the Iroquois. Its leaves, and those of its relative, Purple Bergamot, *Monarda fistulosa*, were used by the Indians to make a tea for chills or fever, or to make a perfume. The plants contain a volatile oil that repels insects, and the dried, powdered leaves were sprinkled on meat to help to preserve it.

Beebalm is found from Minnesota to Ontario and Quebec, south to Tennessee, Georgia and New Jersey. Blooming from July to September, it reaches a height of 2 to 3 feet (60 to 90 cm). It is easily grown from seeds or root divisions in moist locations.

Spotted Saxifrage

Saxifraga bronchialis
ssp. *austromontana*

SAXIFRAGACEAE

It is as if an artist had seized his smallest brush and palette and, with great care, placed a series of round dots on the white petals, progressing from yellow at the base, through orange to bright red. Each tiny flower is a picture deserving magnification so its beauty can be appreciated.

One of the commonest Saxifrages in North America, its range extends from sea level to arctic alpine regions, from Alaska to British Columbia and Alberta and south in the mountains to Oregon and New Mexico. The plant is a small perennial, growing 2 to 6 inches (5 to 15 cm) high, with crowded evergreen leaves and creeping stems that root, forming a mat of plants.

The generic name means rock-breaker, which is true of those species whose roots are thrust down into tiny cracks in rocks, and as the roots grow, the cracks grow, too. The specific name comes from *bronchus*, a branch, referring to the many creeping stems. Other names are Common Saxifrage and Matted Saxifrage.

Sitka Valerian, Mountain Valerian

Valeriana sitchensis

VALERIANACEAE

Moist open meadows and slopes in the mountains are wild gardens usually full of many kinds of flowers in July and August. Valerian is often among them, punctuating the meadow with white or pale pink. Their scent is strong and sweet, said by some to be too strong, and is like that of the garden Heliotrope, *Valeriana officinalis*, a close relative.

The clusters of pink, unopened buds develop into small flowers with very long stamens. The plant blooms from June to September, and may be found from southern Alaska through British Columbia and Alberta, south to California. The leaves of this species are coarsely toothed and opposite, with one to four pairs of lobes. The stem is square and up to 3 feet (90 cm) high in some places.

The generic name is said by one authority to be from the Latin *valere*, to be healthy. According to the Swedish botanist, Linnaeus, it is in honor of Publius Aurelius Valerianus, Emperor of Rome from 253 to 260 AD, who first used a tincture of the root medicinally. Up to the nineteenth century, the plant was used as a mild sedative. The specific name refers to the place, Sitka, where it was first collected about 1833 by F. C. Mertens, a German botanist.

Soapwort, Bouncing Bet

Saponaria officinalis

CARYOPHYLLACEAE

Soapwort has a long and fascinating history. Native to Germany and France, it was brought to England in the Middle Ages by wandering friars, to use as soap. It grew readily in monastery gardens. By the reign of Elizabeth I, when manufactured soap was still unknown, it was valued for cleaning and washing, and had become naturalized in England. Someone with imagination thought the flower suggested the rear view of a woman washing clothes with her petticoats pinned up, bobbing up and down as she scrubbed in a tub of suds made from this plant. Thus, it was named Bouncing Bet.

Later, at the time of the English Industrial Revolution, the roots and leaves were used in preparing the newly-woven cloth to receive the patterns to be stamped on it, becoming known as Fuller's Herb. It would be grown near the factory, on the banks of the mill stream, for convenient gathering.

The plant thrives in disturbed ground and has become naturalized across Canada and throughout most of the United States. Long a garden plant, it is valued for its delicate color, spicy perfume and hardiness. It blooms from July to October and reaches a height of 1 to 3 feet (30 to 90 cm). It is poisonous if eaten, causing severe irritation to the digestive tract.

Common Bladderwort, Greater Bladderwort

Utricularia vulgaris

LENTIBULARIACEAE

This insectivorous plant lives just below the surface of ponds, marshes and the quiet backwater of slow streams. Its long stems radiate outwards; the leaves are modified into branching filaments, to which small oval bladders are attached. The thread-like filaments produce some food for the plant by photosynthesis. The bladders have two functions: one is to buoy the plant up near the surface, allowing the flower stalks to extend 1 to 12 inches (2 to 30 cm) above the water, the other is to capture "food." Most mosquito larvae are too large to enter the bladders, but small water fleas and minute rotifers are lured into them. Once in, the mouth of the bladder is shut fast, and the insect cannot get out. It is slowly digested by enzymes and acid secreted by microscopic glands inside the bladder. Thus, the plant obtains nitrogen not supplied by the water.

Though common and widespread, this plant is usually recognized only when it blooms, which is infrequently. The bright yellow flowers have two lips and a short spur, and may appear from May to September, although the plant requires water at least 2 feet (60 cm) deep to flower. Its range is from Alaska to Newfoundland, and south throughout North America.

Bur-reed

Sparganium species

SPARGANIACEAE

Crowded by other green plants at the fringe of a marsh, the white-balled spires of Bur-reed are often hidden from view. There are more than a dozen species in North America, all similar in appearance. The smaller ones may be only a few inches or centimeters tall; the largest can rise to 6 feet (2 m). All have long, iris-like leaves. Male and female flowers occur on the same plant, and the latter produce a round, greenish, ball-shaped fruit, or bur, with a prickly hull, from which the common name, Bur-reed, has come. In the fall, the fruits fall off, float until water-logged, disintegrate and sink into the wet mud, where the seeds germinate the next spring. These seeds are a favorite food of waterfowl and marsh birds across Canada and the United States.

Pinedrops

Pterospora andromedea

PYROLACEAE

The tall, reddish-brown spikes of the Pinedrops, rising 2 to 3 feet (60 to 90 cm) or more above the forest floor, are among the most impressive summer woodland flowers. There may be forty to sixty pendant, urn-shaped blooms on a single stalk. They range from white to yellow or red in color, and are similar to those of Blueberries. This plant has no true leaves, being parasitic on the roots of other plants, but its very sticky stem is adorned with brownish-red bracts massed near the bottom. The red stems are noticeably attractive in winter.

Pinedrops is the sole member of its genus, which is exclusively North American in distribution. Very rare and local in the east, it is much more evident in the western mountains. It blooms in coniferous, and especially dry pine woods, June to August, from British Columbia to Prince Edward Island, south through the northern United States, and in the Rockies and Sierras to Mexico.

Leafy Thistle, Elk Thistle

Cirsium foliosum

COMPOSITAE

These short or tall leafy plants may be found in cool, wet meadows at low to high elevations in the mountains. While most Thistles have bright pink-purple flowers, Leafy Thistle has white to pale pink ones. In contrast to the prickly stems of many other Thistles, Leafy Thistle is hairy all over, with soft spines that hardly prick at all. Growing to a variable height, from 1 foot (30 cm) to more than 4 feet (120 cm), it is in bloom from June to August. Look for this plant east of the Cascades, from the Yukon through British Columbia and Alberta, south to California and Arizona. It is also found along isolated lime shores in eastern Quebec.

Deer, elk and bear enjoy eating this Thistle, and butterflies come to it in large numbers. When peeled, the stem can be eaten raw and has a pleasant, sweet taste. The root may be peeled and boiled as survival food.

Cirsium is from the Greek name for a kind of plumed Thistle that was used as a remedy for swollen veins, and *foliosum*, meaning leafy, accurately describes this plant.

Birdsfoot Trefoil

Lotus corniculatus

LEGUMINOSAE

One of the most rapidly spreading of introduced plants is the strikingly lovely Birdsfoot Trefoil. Brought in as a forage plant, it has freely escaped from cultivation and now ranges along roadsides, in old fields and waste places from British Columbia to Newfoundland, and across the northern United States, growing from 4 to 10 inches (10 to 25 cm) in height. Its brilliant yellow, sometimes orange or red, blooms, are like Pea blossoms in form, and may occur in great profusion from June to September.

This plant has more than seventy common names in Great Britain alone. Birdsfoot refers to the appearance of its pods, which look as though some strange, multi-toed birds had been walking through the plants. Trefoil, meaning three-parted leaf, describes how the three upper leaflets on each leaf stalk are grouped in a clover-like manner. In the language of flowers in popular use during the nineteenth century, Birdsfoot Trefoil meant "revenge."

Fan-leaf Cinquefoil

Potentilla flabellifolia

ROSACEAE

When the alpine meadows of the western
mountains are in full bloom, this bright flower
adds its color to the palette. It is easily identified by the long-stemmed basal leaves, which
are divided into three leaflets. Each leaflet is
deeply toothed and fan-shaped. The flower
stalk is from 5 to 10 inches (13 to 25 cm) tall.
Most plants of this genus have a great many
stamens, but this flower has only a single
ring of them. It blooms June to September
from British Columbia to Alberta, and south
to Montana and California in the mountains.

Potentilla is a large genus whose name is
from the Latin *potens*, powerful, because some
species were thought to have medicinal power.
Flabellifolia means leaves like small fans.
Cinquefoil is from the old French for five-
leaved, referring to those species with five
leaflets.

Spiderwort

Tradescantia ohiensis

COMMELINACEAE

The prominent flowers of the Spiderwort are a rich violet or deep-rose color and shaped like three-parted, swelling triangles, an inch (2 cm) or more across. They are quick to catch the eye. Occasional white-flowering plants show off the characteristic blue stamen hairs to a great advantage. Spiderwort plants may grow as high as 1 to 4 feet (30 to 120 cm), with long, lanceolate or spear-like leaves that commonly grow taller than the flower cluster. In this species, the flower stems, bracts and leaves are smooth and have a white bloom in contrast to its close relative, *Tradescantia virginiana*, which is hairy on its sepals and flower stalks. Long a garden favorite, this plant is now a common escape in many places beyond its normal range.

It blooms in meadows, damp thickets and woodlands, April to June, from Minnesota, Nebraska and Ontario, east to Massachusetts, and south to Florida and Texas.

Purple Mariposa Lily, Butterfly Tulip

Calochortus macrocarpus

LILIACEAE

The exquisite coloring and size of the flowers of these Lilies led early explorers and plant collectors to vie with one another to give them names reflecting their beauty. Thus, while *Calochortus* means pretty grass, some of the species are named *elegans*, *superbus* and *splendens*. This species, *macrocarpus*, is named for its large seed. Butterfly Tulip is translated from the Spanish, *mariposa*, for butterfly.

The sixty-odd species of Mariposas in western North America bloom in white, yellow, pink or purple, marked at the base of each petal with other colors. The crisp, sweet bulbs of this species and of several others were an important element, raw or cooked, in the diets of many Indians. They were dug in the spring, before flowering.

Mariposas are becoming rare in some places because agriculture is destroying their habitat. Like many of our loveliest flowers, these beautiful Lilies need protection. Look for them from southern British Columbia to northeastern California. They reach 1 to 2 feet (30 to 60 cm) in height, blooming from June to August.

Western Wood Betony, Indian Warrior

Pedicularis bracteosa

SCROPHULARIACEAE

The first plant to be named *Pedicularis* grew in Europe in fields where cattle were feeding. When the cattle became infested with lice, it was assumed that this plant was responsible, so the name *Pedicularis*, meaning little louse, was given to it. Of course, this theory has been discredited for a long time. *Bracteosa* refers to the leafy bracts at the base of each flower stalk.

The many Betonys have been used for centuries to treat almost every illness. They were planted in monastery gardens and in graveyards because they were supposed to drive away evil spirits.

The main stem of this plant can be as tall as 3 feet (90 cm). The showy flowers, which may be red or yellow, grow in an elongated cluster at the top. The upper part of each flower is beaked, narrow and arched. They appear in July and August. The fern-like leaves are alternate on the stalk.

This plant grows in moist woods and open meadows below the tree line in the mountains. Its range is from British Columbia and Alberta south to Montana, Colorado and California.

Rocky Mountain Bee-plant

Cleome serrulata

CAPPARIDACEAE

Easily recognized by its long stamens, its long, drooping seed capsules and its showy pink flowers, Rocky Mountain Bee-plant grows in arid regions, on plains and in the foothills of the mountains. It may be found from southern British Columbia to Manitoba, and south to California, New Mexico and Texas. In other places, such as Ontario and Quebec, it has been introduced. Occasionally, a white-flowered form of this species is seen. The plant is tall, up to 4 feet (120 cm) in height, and blooms from May to August.

It is a favorite with bees, hence its common name, Bee-plant. Other common names are Wild Spiderflower and Stinkweed, the latter name given because of the goat-like scent of the plant. The generic name is ancient, once used by the Greek scientist, Theophrastus, for a mustard-like plant in Europe. *Serrulata* comes from the Latin for a small saw, referring to the finely toothed leaves.

Showy Locoweed

Oxytropis splendens

LEGUMINOSAE

This beautiful member of the Pea family is easily identified, since all its parts, except the purple flowers, are covered with silvery hairs. It grows on grassy slopes, dry, gravelly ground and in open woods, from Alaska to New Mexico, and east to Ontario and Minnesota, blooming from June to August. Its leaves have many leaflets and grow in whorls from the base of the stem. It looks like a small bush, reaching a height of 4 to 16 inches (10 to 41 cm).

Oxytropis is a combination of two Greek words, *oxys*, sharp, and *tropis*, keel. In this species, the keel, made up of the two lower petals, is beaked, although this can only be seen by close examination of the flower. *Splendens* is translated by showy. Locoweed, the English name for members of this genus, comes from the Spanish *loco*, or crazy.

Locoweeds have a bad reputation, since some of them contain a poisonous chemical to which cattle become addicted, and when they have eaten too much, they go mad and die. Showy Locoweed is not one of these plants.

Pickerel Weed

Pontederia cordata

PONTEDERIACEAE

Huge numbers of Pickerel Weed may at times rim an entire shallow pond, forming a blue-topped boundary of green between water and land. These plants grow from 1 to 4 feet (30 to 120 cm) high, and carry lusty stalks of blue flowers from June to November. Impressive as they are at a little distance, the flowering stalks seem patchy at close quarters, as the flowers bloom only a few at once, working from the bottom up, so that there are few spikes fully in bloom. The blue, occasionally white, flowers are six-parted and have two yellow spots at the center. There is usually one thick, dark-green leaf, often arrow-shaped, on the stem, and other heart-shaped leaves at the base of this plant. These plants provide a rich habitat attractive to aquatic insects, and therefore to many fish, hence, the common name. Pickerel Weed is often a favorite food of deer, and has been used as an ornamental in garden pools.

It prefers shallow water and mud and may be found southward to Texas and Florida from Minnesota, Ontario and Nova Scotia.

Sticky Tofieldia, False Asphodel

Tofieldia glutinosa

LILIACEAE

Often growing in masses in the open lime fens, marshes and on the shores it prefers, this plant blooms from June to August, and occasionally into September. Its small, white flowers are bunched at the top of an almost bare stem, which rises 8 to 20 inches (20 to 51 cm) from a group of grass-like leaves.

The chief mark of the plant is its extremely sticky stem, covered with red or black glands, apparently providing protection against the unwanted attentions of certain climbing insects. The reddish capsules of its inedible fruit are pleasing spots of color in late summer.

The plant is found from Alaska across Canada and the northern United States, and south in the east to West Virginia and Georgia. There is a close relative in California.

It was given the name False Asphodel because its flowers resemble those of the old-world Asphodel, a special or magical plant throughout the eastern Mediterranean area from earliest historical times, considered to be among the "lilies of the field" mentioned in the Bible.

Wild Raspberry

Rubus idaeus

ROSACEAE

Hanging like round red jewels on the end of short stalks, this berry is a favorite with animals, birds and people. The plant grows in open, moist woods or fields and on rocky slopes across Canada and the United States, except on the Pacific coast, where this species is replaced by the Black Raspberry, *Rubus leucodermis*. There are several other species across the continent with fruit that is good to eat.

The white-petalled flowers open in June and July, and are followed by the fruit, usually ripening in July and August, but which may be found until September in a favorable year. Raspberries are easy to recognize, for they are made up of a thimble-shaped group of drupelets. The ripe fruit comes off the white receptacle easily — so easily that many berries fall to the ground. The leaves are compound, with three to five leaflets. The long canes or main stems are often thorny, and are usually called brambles or briars. (Peter Rabbit, in Beatrix Potter's beloved stories, lived in the Briar Patch.)

Wild raspberries are delicious fresh or made into pies, jams, jellies or syrup. They freeze and preserve well. Salmonberries and thimbleberries are closely related.

Lamb's Ears, Woolly Hedge Nettle

Stachys olympica

LABIATAE

The pale-purple flowers of Lamb's Ears nestle snugly in the midst of softly white, woolly stems, leaves and bracts. The blooms appear from July to September. Brought to North America by early settlers, the plant has escaped from cultivation and occurs locally in certain areas of Ontario, southwestern Quebec and the northeastern United States. It prefers a rocky, semi-barren habitat similar to its native homeland in the Caucasus Mountains, growing 18 inches to 3 feet (46 to 90 cm) in height.

Its presence here is a good example of the practice of pioneers bringing flowers loved at home across the seas to a new and unknown land for remembrance's sake, and as a gentle antidote to loneliness.

Mountain Globe Mallow

Iliamna rivularis

MALVACEAE

Look for this native wild Hollyhock along mountain streams and in moist meadows in southern British Columbia and Alberta, south to Oregon, Montana, Utah and Colorado. These stout perennial plants grow to a height of 2 to 6 feet (60 cm to 2 m), and bloom from June to August. The pink, purplish or white flowers are large, up to 2 inches (5 cm) in diameter, and grow in a loose raceme at the top of the stem.

The stamens of the flower are arranged in two concentric rings at their base, and form a tube around the club-shaped pistil. The leaves are large and maple-like, with three to seven lobes. Other common names for this species are Mountain Hollyhock and Streambank Rose Mallow.

Mountain Lady's Slipper

Cypripedium montanum

ORCHIDACEAE

One of the many memorable sights of a hike in the western mountains might be a group of Mountain Lady's Slippers in the woods or on a slope along the way. Its range is from British Columbia east of the Cascades to Alberta, and south to California, Montana and Wyoming.

The white slipper is sometimes tinged with purple, and its elegant shape and beauty make this plant one of the loveliest of the Lady's Slippers. The twisted linear petals and the sepals are dark red-brown or purplish-brown. The sterile stamen resembling a shield in front of the column is bright orange-yellow. There are from one to three (usually two) blooms on each stalk rising from the axils of the bracts near the top of the stem. This orchid flowers from May to July, and may reach a height of 30 inches (76 cm). The Mountain Lady's Slipper is rather rare, but in a suitable habitat large numbers may be found. It does not transplant, and will be destroyed if it is picked. Remember its beauty where you saw it, or photograph it — and you will enjoy it forever. Take pictures, not plants.

Little Pipsissewa, Menzies' Pipsissewa

Chimaphila menziesii

PYROLACEAE

In moist, dark coniferous woods, this low evergreen plant may be half hidden by moss, "born to blush unseen." Its range is limited to British Columbia, south in the mountains to California. Its one to three flowers are white or pink-tinged, and held up by red stems of 6 inches (15 cm) or less in height. Creeping root stalks send up these partly woody stems. The leaves are elliptic, very dark green, and look as if polished with a light coating of wax. The flower petals are recurved, exposing the golden-yellow stamens and green pistil. This perennial blooms from June to August.

Chimaphila is from two Greek words meaning winter and loving, a suitable name for an evergreen. *Menziesii* is in honor of Archibald Menzies, a botanist who traveled with Captain George Vancouver on his voyage around the world in 1792 and 1793.

Albert's Penstemon

Penstemon albertinus

SCROPHULARIACEAE

The name of this plant, Penstemon, means five stamens. Sometimes spelled "Pent stemon," the name given by the Swedish botanist, Linnaeus, draws attention to the sterile fifth stamen, which has no pollen. The fifth stamen is usually bearded or hairy, giving rise to another common name, Beard-tongue.

H. W. Rickett, author of *The Wildflowers of the United States*, writes that there are about 230 species of Penstemon in North America. They have showy flowers in vivid shades of red, blue and purple, and a few in yellow or white. In this species, the bright orange-yellow bearded stamen contrasts vividly with the white throat and the flaring blue lobes of the flower.

Albert's Penstemon grows in dry, open places at low and moderately high altitudes. Its range is from southeastern British Columbia to southwestern Alberta and south to Montana and Idaho. Blooming from May to July, it may grow to a height of 16 inches (41 cm).

Many botanists and plant collectors exploring in the West in the late eighteenth and nineteenth centuries found new species. Penstemons were named after many people, but who "Albert" was is not recorded.

Chicory, Blue Sailors

Cichorium intybus

COMPOSITAE

The sky-blue flowers of the Chicory, which may grow from a few inches or centimeters to 5 feet (1.5 m) high, are among the loveliest of early morning sights from June to October. The blue fades quickly in the sunlight to pink or white, and by noon or shortly thereafter the flowers are commonly closed. Chicory has a tall, branching central stalk, with basal leaves like those of the Dandelion, to which it is related. The young leaves have been used for centuries as a salad green and pot herb. Its long tap roots can be dried, roasted, ground and mixed with coffee. In France, this practice has been firmly fixed since the Napoleonic wars, when French coffee supplies were cut off by a British naval blockade.

Native to Europe and Asia, it is cultivated in parts of France, where it is sold as Wild Endive. Chicory grows wild in dry soil in fields, along roadsides and in waste places throughout most of North America.

Nature photographers find shooting the blue blooms faithfully a great challenge.

Western Monkshood

Aconitum columbianum

RANUNCULACEAE

Tall and distinguished would correctly describe the Monkshood. On a stem up to 6 feet (2 m) tall, the dark blue to purple flowers may stand above the other plants around it. The flower is distinctive, both in its shape, and in the hooded effect of the upper sepal. Extending out and over the central parts of the flower, the hood conceals the "face," as would a monk's hood.

Native to the western mountains, it grows at elevations from 5,000 to 10,000 feet (1500 to 3000 m) along streams and in wet meadows. It may be found from British Columbia to California and New Mexico.

The flowers, appearing from June to August, are occasionally white. They require a long-tongued bumblebee to reach their nectary.

Monkshood is a highly poisonous plant in all parts, especially the root. The threat is mainly to livestock, who might wander where it is growing and eat it along with other plants. If eaten by human beings in sufficient quantity, it is fatal. It was used years ago by the Chinese to make a deadly arrow poison, and anthropologist David Nelson, who accompanied Captain James Cook on his third voyage, reported that the people of the Aleutian islands and Alaska peninsula produced an arrow poison from the roots of Monkshood.

Little Blue Penstemon

Penstemon procerus

SCROPHULARIACEAE

These bright blue flowers are usually the color of a northern sky on a clear day, but sometimes they are dark and purplish. There may be one or several crowded whorls of half-inch (1-cm), tubular flowers, which appear from June to August. The sterile fifth stamen, the same length as the fertile ones, is not as visible in this flower as in many of this genus. Basal leaves form rosettes from which a stalk 12 to 24 inches (30 to 60 cm) long grows.

In dry to moist habitats at low to moderate elevations, the range for this flower is from the Yukon to British Columbia and Manitoba, south to California and Colorado. The generic name means fifth stamen, and *procerus* means tall. It is called Little Blue Penstemon because its flowers are small, about .25 inch (6 mm) long. Canadian botanist John Macoun, who travelled west in 1872 before the settlers, remarked on the masses of wildflowers on the prairies, including many Penstemons, which stretched over the horizon in Manitoba.

Marsh St. John's Wort

Hypericum virginicum

HYPERICACEAE

Commonly overlooked in the masses of marsh-edge greens, it comes as a surprise to many naturalists to find a St. John's Wort bearing pink blooms. They grow in the upper leaf axils or at the top of plants that reach 1 to 2 feet (30 to 60 cm) in height, and are followed by the reddish-purple seed capsules later in the summer. The comparatively large, paired and usually clasping leaves are likely to be peppered with translucent dots, and like stems and sepals are often purplish in hue.

The plant blooms in July and August from Manitoba to Newfoundland, south to Nebraska, Illinois, Ohio and Florida. It is one of a considerable number of plants that grow both in eastern North America and in eastern Asia, suggesting that these two continents were once connected by a land bridge in the north.

Purple Honeysuckle

Lonicera hispidula

CAPRIFOLIACEAE

Like most Honeysuckles, this is a climbing or trailing shrub with flowers at the end of the stems in a closely-packed cluster. It climbs on other low shrubs or trails over rocks on dry, open hillsides and shores. The flowers vary from pale pink to purple, and are tubular, with two flaring lobes. The two leaves immediately below the flowers are joined. The lower leaves have distinctive joined stipules, or leaf-like appendages, at the stem, which are a good recognition feature. The plant blooms from June to August on the west side of the Cascade Mountains from British Columbia to California.

Lonicera honors Adam Lonitzer, an early German botanist. *Hispidula* means hairy, which describes the stems of some plants. In days past, Honeysuckle must have been a favorite addition to lovers' bouquets, since in the language of flowers it meant "devoted affection."

Kalm's Lobelia, Brook Lobelia

Lobelia kalmii

CAMPANULACEAE

By the time the little flowers of Kalm's Lobelia decorate the shores of lakes and streams, summer is well on its way. The flowers are distinct from the sky-blue water beyond, because of their purple cast. The white eye in the center of the lower part of each flower is conspicuous but very small in this small bloom. The flowers form a loose spray, or raceme, blooming from bottom to top, July to September. The leaves are narrow, with a few on the stem and others at the base. The roots are usually in shallow water or very wet sand or mud. Growing to a height of 10 to 16 inches (25 to 41 cm), the plants are often in tight bunches.

The genus name, *Lobelia*, is dedicated to Matthias de l'Obel, a Flemish herbalist of the sixteenth century. The species name, *kalmii*, commemorates Peter Kalm, a Swedish botanist who was one of the early plant collectors in North America. He discovered this plant during his extensive travels, perhaps about 1750 when he went to Quebec via the Hudson River, Lake Champlain and the St. Lawrence River. The range of the Brook Lobelia is from British Columbia to Newfoundland and south to Washington, Colorado and New Jersey.

Sea Lungwort

Mertensia maritima

BORAGINACEAE

Sea Lungwort is one of the most attractive of all seaside plants, whether its sleek, powder-blue foliage is streaming across coastal cliffs or rocks, barely out of reach of high tide, or forming elegant mats on sand or gravel beaches. The leaves are thick and succulent with a bloom, adapted to living in a salt-laden atmosphere and habitat. People who have eaten them have said that these leaves taste like oysters, hence the plant's other common name, Oysterleaf. The foliage is far more striking than the flowers, which are pink at first, then turn to blue or white. The plant flowers from June to September.

This seaside *Mertensia* is a close relation of the Virginia Bluebell (*Mertensia virginica*), although very different in look and habitat. Sea Lungwort grows along the seacost from Alaska to Greenland, south to British Columbia on the Pacific shore and Massachusetts on the Atlantic coast.

Showy Milkweed

Asclepias speciosa

ASCLEPIADACEAE

In the western part of North America, this species takes the place of the Common Milkweed, *Asclepias syriaca*. Both species have soft, hairy leaves and milky juice when cut, but Showy Milkweed has larger, showier flowers. They are sweet-scented and very attractive to all butterflies and to other insects, like ants.

Asclepias or *Aesculapius* which is the origin of the generic name, is the name of the Greek god of medicine. The plant was once considered useful medicinally, but is now known to be poisonous, particularly to livestock, when eaten raw. The young shoots are very bitter if eaten raw, but are edible if boiled until tender in several changes of water, each of which must be thrown away. The toxin in the sticky, milky sap is destroyed and discarded with the water.

This annual plant, blooming from May to August, grows to a height of 1 to 4 feet (30 to 120 cm). Its range is from British Columbia to Manitoba and south to California, Missouri and Texas.

Common Foxglove

Digitalis purpurea

SCROPHULARIACEAE

Native to central and eastern Europe, Foxglove spread long ago to other parts of Europe and North Africa. This biennial plant, with its pink-purple bells on tall stalks, was first recorded in North America by John Bartram, an early American plant collector. It was probably planted by English and German colonists in their gardens, since the woolly leaves were used as poultices on persistent sores. Today, a drug derived from a related species of Foxglove is commonly used in the treatment of heart disease.

The plant produces large number of seeds that are distributed by the wind when ripe. Thus, it has spread far beyond gardens and has become naturalized on roadsides and in waste places across Canada and south in the Pacific states. It blooms from May to September, growing to a height of 2 to 6 feet (60 cm to 2 m). There are several species of *Digitalis*, but *purpurea* is the most easily grown. All parts of this plant are bitter and highly poisonous.

In the sixteenth century, it was observed by the Flemish herbalist, Rembert Dodoens, that the plant was common where iron and coal were mined. In some countries today, people in helicopters search for masses of Foxglove to help them find new veins of these minerals.

115

Bladder Campion

Silene vulgaris (cucubalus)

CARYOPHYLLACEAE

The white, deeply divided petals of this little Campion emerge like the arms of an exquisite shellfish from the bladder-shaped calyx. The calyx looks like an exotic shell — smooth, green-brown and beautifully marked with interwoven pink veins. Unhappily, this delicate but persistent and deep-rooted beauty is considered a formidable weed by farmers, able to crowd out cultivated plants and pollute good hay. It comes from Eurasia and is one of the plants that has followed people around the world. Children everywhere amuse themselves by popping the bladders.

It is widespread and thoroughly naturalized on this continent, blooming in fields, along roadsides and in waste places, April to September, from British Columbia to Newfoundland, south to Oregon, Colorado, Kansas, Tennessee and Virginia. It grows 8 to 18 inches (20 to 46 cm) tall.

White Mountain Heather

Cassiope mertensiana

ERICACEAE

In alpine areas close to and above the timber-line, the waxen white bells nod from the tops of the many short branches of this low, creeping shrub. This hardy North American Heather grows very slowly, sprawling over bare rocky areas. It blooms in late July and August, and occasionally is as tall as 12 inches (30 cm). Its range extends from Alaska to British Columbia, east to Alberta and Montana and south in the mountains to California.

Heather is the common name for many plants of the family Ericaceae. For all Scots, this means the Purple Heather of Scotland, *Calluna vulgaris*, and the remark has been made that North American Heathers are not "true heathers." While the plants' names in English could be confusing, there is no confusion at all in their botanical names.

Cassiope was the name given this species by an English botanist, David Don, who continued to choose names from Greek mythology to identify North American plants, as the Swedish botanist, Linnaeus, had done. Cassiopea was the queen of the Ethiopians and mother of Andromeda, for whom another species of Ericaceae had already been named, so it seemed appropriate to use her mother's name for a related species. *Mertensiana* was given to honor F. C. Mertens, a German botanist.

Beach Pea

Lathyrus japonicus

LEGUMINOSAE

This robust member of the Pea family may be found in flower-dotted green masses, scrambling over sand dunes or shingle beaches, or ornamenting the lee side of a stranded log. Its underground stems may grow as long as 20 feet (6 m), making Beach Pea one of the best sand-holding plants that exists. It is quite variable both in foliage and in flower throughout its world-wide distribution so many forms and varieties have been described. The colors of the blooms, though commonly purple, can vary from white to red, and be kaleidoscopic in the same lot of plants. When the pioneers came, they used the peas as food, and learned from the Indians to eat the fresh sprouts and shoots.

Beach Pea blooms June to September. It is circumpolar and grows south from Arctic Canada to California on the Pacific coast, to New Jersey on the Atlantic, and along the shores of the Great Lakes.

Purple-flowering Raspberry

Rubus odoratus

ROSACEAE

It is scarcely surprising that so many people coming upon this plant's conspicuous bloom believe that they have found a new Rose. The flowers are very rose-like, deep red or purplish in hue and, at times, may be as much as 2 inches (5 cm) across. A closer look at the large, maple-like leaves and the branches clad with glandular-clammy hairs, however, will tell the observer that this plant is more closely related to Raspberries than to Roses. Perhaps the most elegant of Raspberries in its flowers, it falls to a low rating in its fruit, which is large, luscious-looking, even edible, but disappointingly insipid, dry, seedy and acid. Purple-flowering Raspberry is valued both in its native North America and in Europe as a garden plant, reaching 3 to 6 feet (1 to 2 m) in height.

It grows at the edges of rocky woods, in ravines and wild hedgerows, from Ontario, Quebec and Nova Scotia, south to Tennessee and Georgia, blooming from June to September.

Autumn

Black Cherry, Rum Cherry

Prunus serotina

ROSACEAE

There is apt to be some confusion between Black Cherry and Chokecherry. At a glance, the leaves, flowers, and fruit look much alike, but on the Black Cherry, there is a fringe of fine brown hairs on the midrib on the underside of the mature leaves. This fringe does not occur on the Chokecherry leaves. On the ripe cherries, which hang in clusters, the shrunken remains of the calyx are visible at the base of the stem of each fruit. On Chokecherry, this bit of calyx is absent.

The small, black cherries are late in ripening and become sweeter as time passes. Birds, chipmunks and squirrels all eagerly dine on them. If there is a good crop, these slightly bitter, though not astringent, cherries can be made into a delicious jelly. Beware of the leaves, bark and pits. All contain hydrocyanic acid and should not be eaten.

This tree may grow up to 70 feet (21 m) in a good location. The wood was once highly prized for furniture, but now is almost unobtainable. It is hard and strong, light to dark red-brown.

Found mostly in the eastern part of North America, this species has long been called Rum Cherry because it was used by early settlers in New England to sweeten and flavor the raw rum they imported from the West Indies.

Smooth Wild Rose,
Meadow Rose (Rose hips)

Rosa blanda

ROSACEAE

In June and July, the lovely scent of wild roses can be recognized from a distance when the sun is warm and the breeze blows from their direction. Many insects are attracted to the bright pink flowers; bees of all kinds feast on the pollen, easily accessible in the open, five-petalled flower. This results in good pollination and abundant rose hips in August, September and October.

These shrubs grow in sandy or rocky soil, in open sunny places, in fields and along roadsides, from Manitoba to Quebec and south from Missouri to Pennsylvania.

Different parts of Wild Roses may be used in many ways. Rose petals may be candied, or picked fresh, they may be added to salads. They have been used for many years to produce rosewater, and were once used to make wine. The young leaves may be dried and used as a tea. In using rose hips, care must be taken to remove the seeds, which have irritating hairs on them. The hips are often combined with lemon juice or other fruit for added flavor to make into jam or jelly, and contain a large amount of Vitamin C.

Prickly Rose, *Rosa acicularis*, is Alberta's provincial flower, and Wild Roses are the floral emblems of Georgia, Iowa and North Dakota.

127

Large Cranberry, American Cranberry

Oxycoccus macrocarpus

ERICACEAE

The large, glossy, red berries on this creeping plant attracted the English explorer Samuel Hearne and his party on their expedition to the Arctic Ocean in the 1770s. He reported that in the area that is now Churchill, Manitoba, the berries were abundant in bogs, muskegs, on plains and rocks. This fruit was gathered in late fall, packed in barrels and covered with water, to be sent back to England.

The plants are evergreen, trailing shrubs, and their thread-like roots are fastened in wet soil or sphagnum moss. The leaves are small and oval, dark green on top and whitish beneath. Blooming in July and August, the tiny flowers are white or pink, with four recurved petals and protruding stamens. The berries ripen late in the year, in October and November, and may be used in any recipe calling for cranberries. Frost seems to sweeten them, and they will last till spring under the snow, providing food for small animals throughout the winter. This species is found from Manitoba to Newfoundland and south to Arkansas and North Carolina.

Commercial cranberries were developed from the Large Cranberry. They are now grown in bogs with controlled water levels, allowing the bogs to be flooded; the ripe berries then float to the surface for harvesting. Cape Cod in Massachusetts is famous for its cranberry bogs.

Wild Grape, Frost Grape

Vitis riparia

VITACEAE

Wild Grapes were often mentioned in the early history of plants native to North America. Several wild species were planted and cultivated, the largest of which was the Frost Grape. In 1670, explorer François Dollier de Casson reported wild grapes growing on the shore of Lake Erie in quantities sufficient to make thirty hogsheads of wine, almost 1900 gallons or 7200 liters!

There are a large number of wild species, mostly in the south and west of North America. All resemble cultivated Grapes. *Vitis riparia* grows from Manitoba to New Brunswick and Nova Scotia, and south to Texas. Along roadsides and in thickets of small trees, the vines will cling to any support with their strong tendrils. The flowers, blooming in May and June, are small and greenish. They may be perfect (bisexual) or monosexual. The leaves are large and broad, with three to five lobes. In October, the black grapes, which look blue because of a bloom, hang from their support, as in an arbor. They are best and sweetest after a frost.

Delicious jelly can be made from the fruit. The jelly will set without pectin if a few unripe grapes are mixed with the ripe ones.

Staghorn Sumac (Fruit)

Rhus typhina

ANACARDIACEAE

The Staghorn Sumac, a small tree that grows from 6 to 30 feet (2 to 9 m) tall, received its common name because in the winter, its angling, bare branches, covered with fuzzy hairs, look like the velvety antlers of male deer. The clusters of spring flowers, greenish-white, loose and open on male plants, smaller, more compact and with a hint of red on female plants, are so small that they are often overlooked. The large, cone-shaped, tightly-packed clusters of small fruits, covered with red hairs, stay on the tree all winter. They can be used in jellies or lemonade, or are a good source of food for many birds and animals. For early spring migrants, like robins and bluebirds, they can be life-saving when late snowstorms rage.

Staghorn Sumac grows in sunny fields sandy, gravelly and rocky areas, and at the edges of woods from Ontario, Quebec and Nova Scotia, south to Minnesota, Iowa, Kentucky and North Carolina. It blooms in June, with its hairy red fruit ripening in July and August. Its compound leaves turn a brilliant scarlet or crimson in fall, making an outstanding contribution to the autumnal show.

Common Milkweed (Seeds)

Asclepias syriaca

ASCLEPIADACEAE

For many annual plants and some biennials, the way in which their seeds are distributed is important. Over millenia, different methods have evolved. Seeds within fruits may be eaten by birds or mammals and excreted in another place. Some seeds, like Burdock seeds, are covered with hooks that catch in the clothing of people and in the fur of animals and are carried away, to be brushed off in a new location. Distribution by the wind is one very efficient method, to which the Common Dandelion bears witness. Common Milkweed also uses this method. When the green pods containing the closely-packed seeds and their silk plumes split open in late summer and autumn, Milkweed seeds unfurl their parachutes and sail away. On a very windy day, the air above a field of Milkweed may be supporting an army of gliding seeds. Only a few seeds are carried a long distance. The remaining ones will settle near the plant and increase the population of Milkweed in that field.

Though the Common Milkweed is considered a weed by farmers, it is a welcome sight on roadsides and in waste places across eastern North America, as far west as Manitoba and south to Georgia and Kansas. The plant reaches a height of 3 to 6 feet (1 to 2 m).

Moth Mullein

Verbascum blattaria

SCROPHULARIACEAE

Tall and elegant, the often 5-foot (1.5 m) spires of Moth Mullein are crowned in their upper half with bright yellow or creamy-white blooms. Each flower is decked with tufted violet stamens, and the plant seems very much the aristocrat in comparison with its more humble relative, the Common Mullein. The delicate, thin leaves of this plant also contrast with the coarse, woolly, mitten-like leaves of its relation. It has been called Moth Mullein since Roman days, either because the flowers have been thought to resemble moths, or to provide protection against such insects. It was brought to this continent both for its beauty and for its supposed medicinal value. Now, it has found a natural home in our old fields, dry meadows and pastures and along roadsides, blooming June to October, from Ontario and Quebec, south throughout most of the United States.

Common Mullein

Verbascum thapsus

SCROPHULARIACEAE

This sun-loving plant will only develop in the most open, dry places, such as fields, waste places and along roadsides. It is a biennial, setting an impressive rosette of large, gray-green, fuzzy leaves the first year and sending up a tall, thick stem, 2 to 7 feet (60 cm to 2 m) high, topped by a flowering spike, in the second year. The showy, yellow flowers bloom from June to September, and only a few each day, so that the spike is never fully covered. The name, Mullein, means soft, and is very apt for a plant that is soft and woolly all over. Another common name is Flannel-plant.

Mullein has a long history of human use, from the days when Roman ladies used its juices as a hair dye, to the time when young Quaker women, forbidden real rouge, rubbed their cheeks with its leaves to give themselves a stylish flush. For centuries, it was used in herbal medicines. The seeds of this vigorous plant may lie in the ground for more than twenty years and still germinate when full light falls on them. This introduced plant is common across most of Canada and the United States.

133

Highbush Cranberry
Viburnum trilobum
(syn. opulus var. americanum)

CAPRIFOLIACEAE

Conspicuous both in bloom and in fruit, this is one of the most prized of flowering shrubs, growing to 14 feet (4 m) in height. From May to July, the shrub is covered with prominent, flat, circular heads of white flowers. Each head bears an outer ring of striking but sterile blossoms, and an inner core of small, fruitful flowers. Its leaves are maple-like and usually three-lobed, as the previously-used species name, *trilobum*, indicates. The fruit is of a brilliant scarlet color and remains on the shrub all winter, providing food for birds and animals. It can be used for making preserves and jellies, having a flavor similar to, but somewhat more bitter than, cranberries. The berries become translucent and more juicy if they are frozen, and their flavor is improved.

The garden Snowball Bush, which has sterile flowers covering the full heads, has been developed from a closely related European species.

The Highbush Cranberry grows in damp woods, bushy fields and on rocky slopes and shores, from British Columbia to Newfoundland, south to Washington, Wyoming, Iowa, Pennsylvania and New Jersey.

American Bittersweet, Climbing Bittersweet

Celastrus scandens

CELASTRACEAE

Bittersweet is best known for its magnificent red-orange fruit, one of the glories of autumn. In the late fall, the orange capsules split open and reveal the vivid scarlet or crimson covering of the seeds. These fruits are great favorites in winter bouquets, but have been so intensively picked that this plant is now on the endangered list in some places. Left on the vines, the fruit makes a wonderful showing amidst winter snows.

The shrubby Bittersweet vine may grow from 6 to 50 feet (2 to 15 m) in length, and has been seen entirely covering good-sized trees. This characteristic explains its other common name, Climbing Bittersweet. The tiny greenish-white flowers, which appear in late May and June, are scarcely noticed, and rarely associated with the brilliant fall fruit.

Bittersweet is found at the edges of woods, on stream banks and in hedgerows and bushy fields, from Manitoba to Quebec, south to Oklahoma, Louisiana and Georgia.

Yellow Mountain Avens (Seeds)

Dryas drummondii

ROSACEAE

The Yellow Mountain Avens, or Yellow Dryas, makes its home on calcareous cliffs and rocky slopes in arctic and alpine areas. Its range is from Alaska through the mountains of British Columbia and Alberta south to Oregon, Idaho and Montana. It may be found in isolated places north of Lake Superior in Ontario, near James Bay in Quebec and in Newfoundland. This plant is well adapted to the rigorous climate of its habitat, with thick, tough evergreen leaves, densely hairy on the underside, deep anchoring roots, and just enough stalk to display its bright flowers to the insects. Its seeds mature by early fall, and are blown around by the wind.

Dryas is from the Greek for the wood nymph or dryad, to whom the Oak was sacred. The small leaves resemble some kinds of Oak leaves. *Drummondii* is after Thomas Drummond, a botanical collector who was sent to North America by botanist William J. Hooker of Glasgow in the early 1830s, and discovered the plant in the Canadian northwest.

136

Common Thistle, Bull Thistle (Seeds)

Cirsium vulgare

COMPOSITAE

Arriving unannounced and unwanted, this bold invader from overseas has rampaged across North America. Perhaps that is why it is commonly called the Bull Thistle. It is a formidable plant, heavily built, 2 to 6 feet (60 cm to 2 m) tall, and powerfully armored with spines. These spines appear on the upper surface of the large, deeply-scalloped leaves, the only Thistle where this occurs, as well as on the edges of the decurrent leaf structures. These downward projections widen the stem, giving it a "winged" appearance. On the flower bracts, the spines are yellow-tipped. The opening buds gleam like exotic medallion shields, framed in encircling spears of green, and the large red-purple flowers are about 1.5 inch (4 cm) across. In the fall, its seeds travel the countryside on shining, silken parachutes.

Common Thistle blooms in fields, along roadsides and in waste places from June to October, across Canada and the United States.

Panicled Aster

Aster simplex

COMPOSITAE

This tall, sturdy Aster, often growing in dense colonies, is common in damp, open places, meadows and along tidal shores. Flower heads are numerous and are borne in panicles, or clusters, on freely-forking branches. The flowers appear from August to October, and each flower head has two different kinds of flowers. The white ray flowers, which may be tinged with purple, number from twenty to forty, and the whole flower head is about an inch (2 cm) across. The tubular disc flowers in the center of each head are yellow, each having five teeth. The larger leaves are willow-like and smooth, usually with few or no teeth, and there are many small, toothless leaves on the flowering branches. It is, however, a variable plant, so that differences in details are to be expected.

There are many species of white Asters and it is sometimes difficult to tell them apart, but they all add a certain delicacy to the autumnal scene they decorate.

Panicled Aster is found from Saskatchewan to Newfoundland south to Texas, Missouri, Kentucky and North Carolina.

Fringed Grass of Parnassus

Parnassia fimbriata

SAXIFRAGACEAE

With its handsomely fringed petals, this is the most elegant member of the *Parnassia* genus. The flowers are about an inch (2 cm) across, and the creamy-white petals, which appear July to September, have green or yellow veins. It grows about a foot (30 cm) high, up from a good-sized cluster of large, shiny, roundish or heart-shaped basal leaves. The flowering stem is bare, except for a small, clasping leaf, not far below the blooms. Though seemingly fragile, the plant thrives under exacting subalpine and alpine conditions, sometimes gracing boggy areas, brook banks and other wet places at altitudes well over 9,000 feet (2,700 m). Though it may be seen at lower elevations, it is one of the botanical prizes sought by mountain-climbing naturalists in the western mountains.

It grows from Alaska south to northern California, and east to Colorado and Alberta.

Hairy Gooseberry, Canada Gooseberry

Ribes oxyacanthoides var. *hirtellum*

SAXIFRAGACEAE

In a good season, this low shrub may be laden with fruit. The berries are dark red-purple, sweet and seedy when they ripen in August and September. The bushes are found from Manitoba to Newfoundland, and south to Pennsylvania in moist woods and dry rocky areas. They grow to a height of 3 feet (1 m). The three- to five-lobed deciduous leaves are soft and hairy underneath. There are usually thorns at the nodes and on the lower branches. The small flowers, blooming from May to July, have greenish-yellow, reflexed petals and protruding stamens.

There are several other species of Gooseberry growing in Canada and the United States. Unfortunately, some *Ribes* species are host to the White Pine blister rust, which damages and kills White Pine and some western pines. For this reason, many Wild Currants and Gooseberries, which are all in the genus, have been destroyed.

Some species of Currants are grown in gardens for their lovely flowers, the most spectacular of which is the Red-Flowering Currant of British Columbia. Wild gooseberries may be eaten raw, but are usually better when cooked. They make good jam and excellent jelly.

Western Anemone (Seeds)

Anemone occidentalis

RANUNCULACEAE

Called Wind Flower, Towhead Babies and Old Man of the Mountains by those who frequent alpine meadows, it is most conspicuous when the seeds ripen, because the stalk of the seedhead lengthens.

The white flower, with their ring of close-ranked stamens, bloom from June to September. They may be seen in rocky alpine areas, often as soon as the snow melts. Some seedheads are ripe in early August, and the seeds may be carried a fair distance, supported by their feathery tails.

Anemone comes from the Greek, *anemos,* meaning wind. Pliny the Elder, a Roman scholar and naturalist (c. AD 23–79) wrote in his *Historia Naturalis* that Anemones opened only at the bidding of the wind. The range of this plant stretches from British Columbia to Alberta, south to northern California, Idaho and Montana, at middle to high elevations in the mountains.

Hoary Vervain

Verbena stricta

VERBENACEAE

Sandy fields, prairies and old, dry pastures where cattle have spurned its bitter-tasting foliage are likely places to look for this wild relative of the garden Verbenas. It grows from Washington and Montana to southern Ontario, farther east where it has become naturalized, and south to New Mexico, Tennessee and Texas. Closely related to the Blue Vervain, it may be distinguished by its larger, more purplish and sometimes pink flowers, which grow in blunt-ended upright spikes. They bloom from June to September.

Its common name, Hoary Vervain, has been given because its coarse-toothed leaves, stems and floral bracts are densely covered with soft, white hairs. The plant may attain a height of almost 4 feet (120 cm).

Blue Vervain

Verbena hastata

VERBENACEAE

The tall, branching Blue Vervain grows in wet places throughout most of Canada and the United States. Usually reaching 3 to 6 feet (1 to 2 m) in height, the plants are topped by compact clusters of slender flowering spikes. These pointed spikes, appearing from June to October, bear a large number of small, five-petalled flowers, though only a few are likely to be open at one time, creating patches or circles of bloom on the spike. They are normally of a violet-blue color, but may be pink or white. Four-sided stems and lanceolate, or spear-shaped, toothed leaves are typical, but sometimes the lower leaves are hastate, or arrow-shaped, giving rise to the species name, *hastata*. This plant was used both by the Indians and the settlers as a folk medicine or simple (an herbal remedy), and is sometimes known as Simpler's Joy.

Herb Robert

Geranium robertianum

GERANIACEAE

The small, unnotched, pink or roseate flowers of this little Geranium dot the edges of many woodlands. Eight inches to 2 feet (20 to 60 cm) high, the plant is likely to be strong smelling because of a resinous secretion common to Geraniums.

The plants have compound, triangular-shaped leaves made up of three to five leaflets that are fern-like in appearance, with the end leaflet clearly stalked. The stem, and often the foliage, tend to be reddish in color. Herb Robert has the typical Geranium fruit, candle-like in form, which bursts open when ripe like a released spring, throwing and effectively dispersing the seeds.

The plant blooms in rocky woods, cold ravines and along stream banks, May to October, or until the frost, from Manitoba to Newfoundland, south to Nebraska, Indiana, West Virginia and Maryland.

Grass of Parnassus

Parnassia glauca

SAXIFRAGACEAE

The cream-toned cups of the Grass of Parnassus, green-veined and yellow-centered, can turn sweeping reaches of open meadows and bog into a realm of unbelievable beauty. This species of *Parnassia* may attain a height of 2 feet (60 cm). Its stem is bare, except for a small leaf about midway up; a group of thick, round, oval or heart-shaped leaves grow at its base. The leaves are blue-green, hence its species name, *glauca*. The plants in no way resemble grass, nor is this species in any way a Grass. Its common name goes far back into the ancient past, when the people thought many plants were fit for the gods, Apollo and Dionysius, of Mount Parnassus in Greece. The term "grass" was used in a general way, much as we use the word "plant" today.

Look for the flowers from July to October in open, wet, lime-rich meadows, bogs and on prairies from Saskatchewan to Newfoundland, south to South Dakota, Iowa, Ohio and New Jersey.

Dwarf Goldenrod, Grey Goldenrod

Solidago nemoralis

COMPOSITAE

Gregarious by nature, this Goldenrod may sweep in tides over dry hillsides and slopes. It is certainly one of the commonest of the Goldenrods, yet it is often passed by because of its humble manner of growth. It is nearly always bent over, keeping a low profile. This and its rather one-sided yellow sprays of flowers conceal its height, which may be from 10 inches to 3 feet (25 to 90 cm) high. The whole appearance is one of modest grace. The larger leaves at the base may be toothed, the increasingly smaller ones up the stem are usually entire and are commonly accompanied by tufts of tiny leaves in their axils. Both leaves and stems are closely covered with fine grey hairs, hence the other common name of Grey Goldenrod.

Dwarf Goldenrod blooms in dry, sandy or clay fields, open woods and on hillsides, June to December, from Alberta to Quebec, south to Arizona, Texas and Florida.

Bibliography

Allan, Mea. *Darwin and his Flowers*. New York: Taplinger, 1977.

Anderson, A. W. *How We Got Our Flowers*. New York: Dover Publication, 1966.

Angier, Bradford. *Field Guide to Edible Wild Plants*. Harrisburg, Pa.: Stackpole Books, 1974.

The Audubon Society Field Guide to North American Wildflowers: Eastern Region. New York: Knopf, 1979.

The Audubon Society Field Guide to North American Wildflowers: Western Region. New York: Knopf, 1979.

Brown, Annora. *Old Man's Garden*. Sidney, B.C.: Gray's Publishing, 1970.

Budd, A. and K. Best. *Wild Plants of the Canadian Prairies*. Ottawa: Queen's Printer, 1964.

Clark, Lewis J. *Wild Flowers of British Columbia*. Sidney, B.C.: Gray's Publishing, 1973.

Cormack, R.G.H. *Wild Flowers of Alberta*. Edmonton: Hurtig, 1977.

Crockett, Lawrence J. *Wildly Successful Plants: A Handbook of North American Weeds*. New York: Macmillan, 1977.

Durant, Mary. *Who named the Daisy? Who named the Rose?* New York: Dodd, Mead, 1977.

Eifert, Virginia L. *Tall Trees and Far Horizons: Adventures and Discoveries of Early Botanists in America*. New York: Dodd, Mead, 1965.

Everard, Barbara and Brian D. Morley. *Wild Flowers of the World*. New York: Crescent, 1970.

Fernald, Merritt, L. *Gray's Manual of Botany*. 8th ed. New York: American Book Co., 1950.

Fitter, R., A. Fitter and M. Blamey. *The Wild Flowers of Britain and Northern Europe*. London: Collins, 1974.

Gibbons, Euell. *Stalking the Wild Asparagus*. New York: McKay, 1962.

_____. *Stalking the Healthful Herbs*. New York: McKay, 1966.

_____. *Stalking the Good Life*. New York: McKay, 1974.

Gleason, Henry A. *The New Britton and Brown Illustrated Flora of Northeastern United States and Adjacent Canada*. New York: New York Botanical Gardens, 1952.

Greenaway, Kate. *Language of Flowers*. New York: Avenel, n.d.

Hardin, James W. and Jay M. Arena, M.D. *Human Poisoning from Native and Cultivated Plants*. 2nd ed. Durham, N.C.: Duke University Press, 1974.

Haughton, Claire Shaver. *Green Immigrants: The Plants that Transformed America*. New York: Harcourt, Brace, Jovanovitch, 1978.

Hitchcock, D. Leo, Arthur Cronquist, Marion Ownbey and J.N. Thompson. *Vascular Plants of the Pacific Northwest*. 5 vols. Seattle: University of Washington Press, 1964–1969.

Klimas, J.E. and J.A. Cunningham. *Wildflowers of Eastern America*. New York: Knopf, 1974.

Luer, Carlyle A. *The Native Orchids of the United States and Canada, Excluding Florida*. New York: New York Botanical Gardens, 1975.

Lyons, C.P. *Trees, Shrubs and Flowers to Know in British Columbia*. rev. ed. Toronto: J.M. Dent, 1965.

Macoun, John. *Autobiography of John Macoun, Canadian Explorer and Naturalist*. Ottawa: Ottawa Field Naturalists, 1979.

Marie-Victorien Sr. *Flore laurentienne*. Montreal: University of Montreal Press, 1964.

Moss, E.H. *Flora of Alberta*. Toronto: University of Toronto Press, 1959.

North, Pamela. *Poisonous Plants*. London: Blandford Press, 1967.

Orr, Robert I. and Margaret C. Orr. *Wildflowers of Western North America*. New York: Knopf, 1974.

Peterson, Lee. *A Field Guide to Eastern Edible Wild Plants*. Boston: Houghton Mifflin, 1978.

Petrie, William. *Guide to the Orchids of North America*. Vancouver: Hancock House, 1981.

Polunin, Oleg. *Flowers of Europe: A Field Guide*. London: Oxford University Press, 1969.

Porsild, A.E. *Rocky Mountain Wild Flowers*. Ottawa: National Museum of Canada, 1974.

Rickett, Harold William. *Wild Flowers of the United States*. 6 vols. New York: McGraw-Hill, 1966.

Saunders, Charles Francis. *Western Wildflowers and their Stories*. New York: Doubleday Doran, 1933.

Scoggan, H.J. *The Flora of Canada*. 4 vols. Ottawa: National Museum of Natural Sciences, 1978–1979.

Slack, Adrian. *Carnivorous Plants*. Cambridge, Mass: The Massachusetts Institute of Technology Press, 1980.

Smith, A.W. *A Gardener's Book of Plant Names*. New York: Harper and Row, 1963.

Smith, Helen V. *Michigan Wildflowers*. Bloomfield Hills, Michigan: Cranbrook Institute of Science, 1961.

Soper, James H. and Margaret L. Heimburger. *Shrubs of Ontario*. Toronto: Royal Ontario Museum, 1982.

Turner, Nancy J. *Food Plants of the B.C. Indians*. Parts 1 and 2. Victoria: B.C. Provincial Museum, 1975 and 1978.

_____ and F. Szczawinski. *Wild Coffee and Tea Substitutes*. Ottawa: National Museum of Natural Sciences, 1978.

_____. *Edible Wild Fruits and Nuts of Canada*. Ottawa: National Museum of Natural Sciences, 1979.

_____. *Wild Green Vegetables of Canada*. Ottawa: National Museum of Natural Sciences, 1980.

Whittle, M. Tyler. *The Plant Hunters*. New York: Chilton, 1970.

Index of Flowers by Common Name

Index of Flowers by Botanical Name